To Frank & Cheryl Beth

With appreciation for both of you and special thanks for your interest and help while this was being written, Frank.

Craig

Psalm 37:3-5

LONELINESS

LONELINESS

The search for intimacy

CRAIG W. ELLISON

CHRISTIAN HERALD BOOKS
Chappaqua, New York 10514

We gratefully acknowledge permission to reprint from the following:

Herbert G. Zerof, *Finding Intimacy* (New York: Random House, 1978).

Communication: Key to Your Marriage (Regal Books) by H. Norman Wright.
© Copyright 1974 Gospel Light Publications, Glendale, California 91209. Used by permission.

Louis McBurney, *Every Pastor Needs a Pastor*, copyright © 1977, p. 64; used by permission of WORD BOOKS, PUBLISHERS, Waco, Texas 76703.

Becky Wilson, *Is Loneliness Necessary? Contempo* magazine, March 1977, p. 29. Used by permission of Woman's Missionary Union, Southern Baptist Convention.

T. S. Eliot, "The Cocktail Party," from *T. S. Eliot: The Complete Poems and Plays*, Copyright 1971, Harcourt, Brace & World. Used by permission.

John Bowlby, *Separation: Anxiety and Anger* (New York: Basic Books, 1973). Used by permission.

Holy Bible: New International Version, Copyright © 1978 by the New York International Bible Society. Used by permission of Zondervan Bible Publishers.

Library of Congress Cataloging in Publication Data

Ellison, Craig W.   1944-
  Loneliness: The Search for Intimacy
  1. Loneliness. 2. Intimacy (Psychology)
I. Title.
BV4911.E56   248.8'6   79-55681
ISBN 0-915684-57-8

MEMBER OF
EVANGELICAL CHRISTIAN
PUBLISHERS ASSOCIATION

Christian Herald, independent, evangelical and interdenomination-
al, is dedicated to publishing wholesome, inspirational and religious
books for Christian families. "The books you can trust."

LONELINESS

CONTENTS

PREFACE

A wide variety of people will find this book helpful. Those suffering from loneliness, their family or friends, pastors, and professional counselors should all gain new insight into the roots and relief of loneliness. The book is written to provide an in-depth analysis of various causes of loneliness for the pastor, professional, or curious lay person. At the same time it provides illustrations, facts, and suggested steps for handling the problem of loneliness that anyone will find beneficial. The book can be read straight through, or it can be read selectively. Those who are currently feeling lonely, or needing suggestions on how to help someone who is, may wish to skip to Part 2 first and come back to Part 1 for a more leisurely reading of my analysis of the major causes of loneliness. Names used in the book are pseudonyms.

I first became involved in the study of loneliness as a result of a former student's influence. For several years I had been doing research, writing and thinking on such topics as interpersonal trust, self-esteem, alienation, and urban need. When Pebble Messamore Praman first approached me I wasn't too interested, but as I thought about it I realized that loneliness was very much related to all of these topics. During the past three years I have been engaged in several studies of loneliness involving over 400 people. At the time that we began there were only four or five books on loneliness, and a comparative handful of articles. Today the problem is talked about practically everywhere, as the experience of crippling loneliness has become part of millions of lives. Conversations with people in Canada and Europe have revealed a similar surge of concern.

I'm greatly appreciative to a number of people for their varied forms of influence and input. To Pebble for turning my concern in this direction. To Ray Paloutzian, my congenial colleague, friend, and co-author on several professional papers, for dialogue, suggestions, and support. To Jim Dobson for his encouragement to write for a more "popular" audience. To former students Ricky Campise, Jean Sangster, Dan Hall, Rita Kinsman, Dean Smith, Cathy Gast, Diane Roper, Amy Jordan, Patty Ward, Tracey Walters, Lisa Mosbaugh, Cheryl Conrad, and Jill Hinkle for their curiosity, desire to learn, perseverance, and contributions through research. To Ann Peplau and Dan Perlman for their encouragement and invitation to be part of the UCLA Research Conference on Loneliness. To Bruce Trotter for help in obtaining volunteers, and Jim and Sue Keith in overseeing one research project conducted by Westmont College students in San Francisco. To Joan Griset and Suzanne Van Wieren for providing some helpful illustrations, and Dave Heffner for suggestions regarding loneliness themes in popular music. Also I'm grateful for the consistent, enthusiastic assistance of Ernest Ettlich, former vice-president for academic affairs at Westmont. His confidence and funding assistance through his office enabled us to progress more quickly than we could have otherwise. To Joyce Thomas for her knowledgeable insights into the experience and needs of widows, and Alexandra Cole for her encouragement and perspectives on a variety of issues. To Paul Heckman, my good friend, for his valuable assistance in data analysis.

The Fairmede Neighborhood Church of the Christian and Missionary Alliance graciously provided space for me to "hide away'' while writing the book. Without this help the process would have been much more difficult.

Simpson College provided substantial secretarial assistance and encouragement through the auspices of David Lambert, business manager. Kathy Penner and Judith Steinmetz cheerfully and competently typed portions of the manuscript, and Jackie Easley duplicated and collated numerous copies of it. My thanks to each.

A very special word of thanks goes to the Rev. Frank Smith, who read the manuscript in detail and provided numerous helpful suggestions. Much of the readability of the manuscript is influenced by his counsel, as well as that of the Christian Herald editorial staff.

As I wrote *Loneliness: The Search for Intimacy*, I was once again struck by the wonderful legacy of love and caring that my parents, William and Marilyn Ellison, provided during my childhood, and still express.

Finally, I want to express my deepest appreciation to my wife, Sharon, and my children — Scott, Timmy, and Jon — for making loneliness part of my past, and giving me the daily opportunity to love and be loved by them. Without their understanding and support the book could not have been written.

Part 1

The Roots of Loneliness

1

THE LONELY CROWD

Perspiration poured down the little boy's face; he ran as fast as his legs would carry him. Gasping for breath, wanting to stop, Billy was pushed forward by the sounds of rocks falling around him and the taunting voices, ''We're gonna get you, Billy, we're gonna beat you up!'' His face streaming with tears, Billy managed to make it to his back yard before they could get him. Every day it was the same. Billy was new to the closely knit, small community. Everybody in his class, except him, went to the only church in town. Because of that they taunted and threatened him. As he stood in his yard behind the fence, Billy felt empty and alone inside. The tears continued to come. Nobody wanted him.

Harry woke up with a dull, sick feeling in his stomach. It was time to start another day, but he didn't want to. Nothing seemed to matter. He was here and she was a thousand miles away. He didn't know anybody in this large city. And the people at the university didn't think as he did. They were interested in drinking, sex, and superficial talk. Why had he come here? He longed so much for Betty. It was going to be another six weeks before he could see her. The letters just didn't come often enough. He missed her smile and her touch. Nobody here knew who he was, or cared. He was all alone. It had gotten so bad that he went out and bought a used television set to keep himself company, especially during supper. Supper was so lonely. And the weekends. Harry could hardly stand listening to the country and western station, but he found himself strangely attracted to the melancholy music and words about broken love.

She knew she should say something, but what? She could feel her face getting flushed and her hands perspiring as the introductions proceeded around the room. What would they think of her? Was her hair in place? They probably noticed the mole on her cheek. Why had she agreed to come to the meeting, anyway? Why did she always get so terrified? As she gave her name, Laura felt as though everyone's eyes were boring right through her. All the others were so funny and had witty things to say. Her mind went blank — she couldn't think of anything to say except her name. After an embarrassing pause, the leader of the group turned his attention to the girl next to her.

Ever since she was a little girl, Laura had felt self-conscious when attention was directed toward her. It didn't matter if it was a social gathering, being called on in class, or talking with a boy. She always felt her heart beating faster and was always at a loss for words. She felt others wouldn't like her if they knew what she was really like, or she would say the wrong thing and they'd think she was stupid. She wanted to reach out, to be liked, to be loved. But she was afraid. At times she felt as though she were in prison, unable to break out or to let others in. Except for Mom and Dad and her sister, she felt completely isolated.

Lenore woke with a start. What time was it? Was it Sunday? Where was she? Then she remembered. It was only Wednesday. As she looked at the clock, she saw it was only 1:30 in the afternoon. Time passed slowly. There was so little she felt like doing, so little she could do since she had fallen and broken her pelvis. The nurses were nice, but they were so busy. Lenore felt there was no one she could talk to. No one cared, or really understood — not even the kids. She couldn't blame them. They each had their own families and had to work long hours. She knew they were trying to be kind when they put her in the convalescent home, but it hurt just the same. Now she not only didn't have George to talk to after his death six months ago, but she missed her neighbors. The kids came to visit about once a week for an hour, and her neighbors, Tom and Jill, came every so often. She tried to summon up enough energy to talk with her roommate. But Susan was so strange. She just didn't feel like she could communicate with Susan, who seemed to be senile. It would only be 100 more hours and John, if he didn't have to be out of town, would come with Joyce and the grandkids.

Marie slammed the door in frustration. She couldn't seem to get through to Dick at all. It seemed it really didn't matter to him whether she was there or not. At first she had admired his emotional control, his sharp wit, and his ambitions. But now he never listened to her and was always too busy to spend time just talking. On his free time he either watched television or was busy in community affairs. Even their sexual life had become routine and unsatisfying. Whenever she tried to explain how isolated she felt, he treated her like a child. He made her feel like she demanded too much from him. It was as though she was living with a stranger. She felt all alone, with no one to turn to.

Who's Lonely?

Loneliness is not a new experience for human beings. It appears that God anticipated the pain of loneliness when He created Eve for Adam. "It was not good," He said, "for man to be alone." In those words and in that act of creation, God established the deep need that we have for intimate companionship. Writers such as John Donne have pointed out that "No man is an island entire of itself. . . . Any man's death diminishes me, because I am involved in mankind." T. S. Eliot also commented powerfully on the terror of loneliness when he said that "Hell is oneself, Hell is alone, the other figures in it merely projections."

Loneliness has been one of America's best-kept secrets. Everybody has felt it, but nobody talks about it. It's been a taboo topic. Nevertheless, the word is out — people are lonely, even normal people.

Loneliness seems to have flooded the lives of millions of modern Americans. It's an emotional epidemic. A recent survey of over 40,000 respondents of all ages found that 67 percent of them felt lonely some of the time.[1] Projected nationally, that amounts to over 150 million Americans who have personally experienced loneliness. Another survey found that over 65 percent of widows over age 50 in several major urban areas mentioned loneliness as a significant problem in their lives.[2] United Methodist Men have established a nationwide 24 hour, toll-free telephone line for people wanting to pray with someone. Loneliness is the most frequently mentioned prayer need that they receive. *Contact*, a nationwide crisis intervention telephone network, received over 18,000 calls due to intense loneliness in one recent six month period.

We all feel lonely sometime during our lives. We may call it depression or boredom, or simply feel exhausted or misunderstood. Closer examination often reveals that what we're feeling is loneliness. About 25,000 people recently filled out a survey placed in the Sunday magazine sections of several East Coast newspapers. Psychologists Carin Rubinstein and Phillip Shaver found that 15 percent of the people felt lonely most or all of the time. Only 6 percent said that they never felt lonely. 78 percent felt lonely at least some of the time.[3] Loneliness is a common experience.

For most of us, loneliness is a temporary feeling. It comes and goes. For others, loneliness is like an arm or a leg. It seems to be part of them. They see themselves as lonely and often act in ways which assure their loneliness. They are the chronically lonely people. Usually we have much more patience with those who are only briefly lonely, especially if they have a good reason and aren't too demanding, depressing, or dependent upon us. It's harder for us to understand chronically lonely people. There may not seem to be any reason for their feelings. Why don't they stop feeling sorry for themselves and snap out of it? we may think. We view them as liabilities. We fail to understand them because most of us don't feel lonely for very long.

Loneliness is not X-rated. It's not for adults only. In fact, loneliness may be felt as early as two or three months of age, when a crying baby can be comforted only by being cuddled. At that point the baby may be saying, "Hold me. Reassure me. Let me know I'm not abandoned."

Little kids feel lonely, too. My two-and-a-half-year-old didn't have a label for it, but he felt it. It took him a number of weeks after our move to accept the fact that we *were* home, and that our home in Santa Barbara was no longer home.

Grade school kids feel lonely. They may express it by complaining, "I don't have anybody to play with," during summer vacation. Or they may disclose it in the tears of feeling rejected and unwanted by the other kids in school.

Sometimes we think that teens are immune to loneliness. It seems they couldn't possibly be lonely with all of the activities they're into and the people they're constantly with. And yet several studies suggest that between 25 and 45 percent of American teens experience serious loneliness.[4] This may be due to not liking the new person they see emerging during puberty, social awkwardness with those of the opposite sex, broken communication with parents, feelings that God isn't real any longer, and dating breakups, among other things. Being with people doesn't keep a teen from feeling lonely any more than it does for adults.

The most lonely group of Americans seems to be young adults. Several researchers have found that they are more lonely than the elderly! In part, this is related to the special search for attachment and intimacy that single young adults find themselves in. They're taught that they're supposed to be married by twenty-five or there is something wrong. First-year college students are among the most lonely of all. As Carol put it, "I miss my folks and my sister. I don't have anybody to talk to. I'm just a number here. My roommate doesn't like the same things I do, and she has a different schedule. The kids I've met in classes are okay, but they're just not the same as my friends at home. I feel so homesick and lonely." Carol dropped out halfway through her first semester in college.

Loneliness among middle-aged adults is often more subtle. It may be seen in the alcoholism of a forty-year-old housewife with teenage kids and a husband who is gone constantly in order to climb the ladder of success. It may be seen in the feelings of emptiness that a pastor privately admits to. He has no one to confide in and must often make decisions that some of his key supporters won't agree with. Sometimes loneliness raises its head when the children leave home and spouses discover they have nothing to talk about beyond superficial, safe small talk.

Divorce is another major source of loneliness in the middle years. Increasing numbers of couples married between twenty and twenty-five years, in their forties and fifties, are breaking up. Regardless of how awful being together was, divorce almost always results in bouts of loneliness. Not only do people miss the spouse they couldn't stand, but relatives may stand back in judgment, and "friends" of the former couple cease to be friends for the individuals. Middle adults also have to adjust to the loss of parents. Their deterioration and death often leave feelings of emptiness and loneliness, even when their loss was expected. Somehow, one's world is no longer complete with Mom or Dad gone. It feels as if part of one's self is missing.

For the older adult, loneliness is less easily admitted. This may be in part a generational difference. Today's older adults were reared to be less raw in their disclosing, to put up with hardships. They were not taught to be as focused on their emotions, constantly contemplating their psychological navels, as it were. The largest single contributor to loneliness among the elderly appears to be death of a spouse. This is especially true for relatively new widows or widowers. In addition, how many close friends and how much contact they have with them is important. Contact with children or relatives doesn't seem to be crucial for many of the elderly.[5] In our mobile society, it's quite likely that regular contact with family may have been quite small, so the emotional ties are not as strong as we might think. For many people, retirement from a lifetime of work is a traumatic and lonely time. Old securities and relationships are removed; new roles and friends must be formed. In the midst of a major identity adjustment, it's not uncommon for retirees to feel cut off and isolated.

It is obvious, then, that we're not alone when we feel lonely. In fact, we're standing in an invisible crowd.

Loneliness Is Big Business

Business has been quick to see the potential. Not all singles are lonely, but singles are more often lonely than married people. There are more than 50 million single, divorced, and widowed people in our cities and suburbs. It has been estimated that they have a purchasing power of over 40 billion dollars. Need I say more? Within the past fifteen years, whole new commercial enterprises have sprung up to rid the lonely of their pain (and their money). In one recent year, one hundred thousand singles apartment units were built across the country, most of them in large urban and suburban areas. The very first singles apartment complexes were built in 1964 in Los Angeles. Now it's big business. Singles bars regularly gross over half a million dollars per year. In addition to the drinks, many of these bars have a fee for entrance into the "promised land." As Suzanne Gordon points out, *Playboy* has had a major influence upon the singles business.[6] Hugh Hefner has worked hard to change singleness from a vice to a virtue by showing all the pleasures the swinging single can have in superficial relationships. For most singles, however, the ideal is to ultimately be attached to someone.

Because of this continuing desire, computer matching companies have been doing a brisk business. For prices ranging from $25 to $250 per year, you can have a number of possible matches given to you each month. Sales pitches combine the irresistible charms of the computer with the professional skills of social scientists to assure you the very best matches.

Another matching service promoting intimacy and attachment is called "Interpersonal Support Network." A former business administration professor at UCLA developed Network. For approximately an $80 entrance fee and $10 per month dues, you can become part of a "family" unit. Each "family" is made up of about fifteen people with different interests, backgrounds, and characteristics. Those joining a family must make a minimum commitment of four months, and then may stay, change families, or drop out. To date, about 40 percent of Network members are single, 40 percent divorced, and 20 percent married. Ages range from 20 to 50. About half the members are women.

Newspapers and some national magazines carry substantial numbers of ads aimed at overcoming loneliness, as much as at providing sexual encounters. For example, a recent issue of *The Atlantic* carried ads like the following:
  *Make friends Worldwide through International correspondence.
  *Lonely? Find your lifemate Nationwide. Details $1. Elite...
  *Lonely!! Meet "New" Singles. World...
  *Lonely? Have nationwide friends. Enclose stamp. Exciting...
  *Date-A-Mate. Single, Widowed, Divorced members anxious to meet you. All ages. All areas. Low cost. Unlimited introductions.
Another leading social science magazine, *Psychology Today*, regularly carries similar ads:

*I love you! Does he really mean it? Only a handwriting
expert — a Graphologist — can tell for sure! Graphology is
your SECRET EDGE in understanding others...

*LOST AT LOVE? Recovering from a broken heart is a
painful experience that can last months — even years.
"PRESCRIPTION FOR A BROKEN HEART" is a revo-
lutionary new guide that shows you how to dramatically
reduce the time it takes to recover. ($10).

Those feeling lonely have become increasingly willing to
advertise their needs as well. A recent issue of The Bay Area
Guardian displayed over sixty personal ads like these:

*Shy, attractive, down to earth W/F actress, 23, seeks
friends. If you're a W/M under 30, 5' 8" or over, fit, and a
fellow non-smoker who loves films and cinema history,
I'd like to meet you. I'm an East Coast escapee who's
travelled in England and Scotland. I'm 5' 5" have fair hair,
blue eyes. I like moustaches, books and red wine. I'm
mainly looking for a friend and companion at the movies
and theater, but if the chemistry's right, who knows?

*Slim, fairly attractive, non-sexist male, late 20's, seeks a
slim attractive bright woman in her 20's, who also dislikes
"singles scene" atmosphere and who seeks intimacy based
on respect, companionship, and monogamous hedonism.

*Casting... for leading man in my life. Smart, sweet, sensi-
tive professional man (a la Richard Dreyfuss, George Segal,
as types go) with zest for living and loving, to play opposite
bright, attractive, well-traveled 35 year W/F attorney-to-be,
recently transplanted from The Big Apple and seeking roots.

*The Greatest Compliment to me by a woman was the state-
ment that I was the MOST non-chauvinistic man she had
ever met. Unfortunately, she was not committed to a long
term relationship with a future. I am seeking a caring
relationship with a non-smoking, very attractive, extremely
sensual, highly intelligent, quite independent, well
proportioned, high energy woman under 36 years of (mental

and physical) age who has a strong sense of self, is able to laugh easily, and is free of traditional sexist expectations vis-a-vis her friend/lover. You are offered intellectual stimulation, mutual respect, open honesty, adequate "space," human closeness, growth reinforcement, emotional support, sexual gratification, ideological compatibility, a wide range of fun activities (flying, sailing, etc.) and, a very busy, high-energy, well-educated, financially secure, 5' 10", 167 lbs., attractive, sensitive, intelligent, huggable, humorous/serious, 44 year old man...

Superman, anyone?

Another part of the loneliness business is the Human Potential Movement. Spawned by psychologists in the late 1940s, the movement has been taken over by a variety of gurus. Each guru has a slightly different path to the "promised land" of inner release and joyful intimacy. The basic purpose is to help people to open up their inner feelings to themselves and others. The theory is that through intensive encounters with others in special small groups, we will become more fully human. In addition, we will build bridges of understanding and trust that will end loneliness. Encounter groups teach followers to live in the present, to be open and honest about feelings and expectations, and to adapt to change. They do these things through a variety of exercises such as the trust walk, two-person confrontation, and touching.

The Human Potential Movement has caught on with millions of Americans in the 1970s. Part of the attraction is the promise of success. No long, drawn out therapy is necessary. Encounter groups are for healthy people who want to grow, not for disturbed people. You might even meet someone in your group with whom you'll gain instant intimacy.

Springing from the more respected encounter group movement have been a number of mass movements led by highly charismatic conquerors of failure. Some of them have religious overtones. These include Guru Maharaj Ji, leader of the Divine

Light Mission, who offers an end to loneliness by becoming part of a mass following with cosmic purposes. Sun Myung Moon's Unification Church has also attracted a large following among young adults searching for a place to belong and a purpose to life. Though close human attachments are actively discouraged, loneliness is overcome by self-sacrifice and absorption into a group. Moon now oversees a multi-million dollar religious enterprise.

Other groups have no religious connections. The most successful is Erhard Seminars Training (est), begun in San Francisco in 1971 by an ex-used car salesman. There are now over 30,000 graduates who have paid a $200 to $250 admission fee to sit through sixty hours of encounter, attack, and other psychological techniques all rolled together into one. There are post-training seminars that members can attend for an additional fee.

Finally, there's the music industry. Labels like Columbia, MCA, and RCA grossed over $3 billion in record and tape sales in 1978. Many hit songs over the years lament lost love, yearning for a lover, or the intimacies of a love relationship. Among bestsellers, for example, were "Without You" (Harry Nilsson), "I'm So Lonely I Could Cry" (Hank Williams), "Ballad of a Lonely Man" (Alan Parsons), and the "Yes Blues" (Beatles). "One is the Loneliest Number" (Harry Nilsson) lamented:

One is the loneliest number that you'll ever do.

Two can be as bad as one, but the loneliest number is the number one.

The rise of "discomania," which has become a $4 *billion* industry, with 12,000 new clubs opened between 1975-77, is at heart due to the appearance of intimacy. The lonely person can find himself on the dance floor, milling around with hundreds of others, being swept up in the music and movement, being physically close to others and making intimate motions without the risk of exposure and rejection.

Why Are People Lonely?

Asking why people feel lonely is somewhat like asking how to get to New York City. Just as there are many roads leading to New York, there are many paths to the experience of loneliness. Two people may feel equally lonely but have quite different precipitating or triggering events for their loneliness.

People who are *chronically* lonely, or feel frequently lonely over a long period of time, find it difficult to make or to keep close friends. Many are shy. They lack confidence in themselves and find making contact with others very painful. Often this is because they are afraid that others won't like them. They may feel that others are watching their every move, rating them on an approve/disapprove scale. This kind of thinking creates tremendous anxiety which shy people often relieve by withdrawing from other people. They become people avoiders. Such a strategy relieves one set of problems but creates another. Anxiety is traded for loneliness.

Other chronically lonely people are not intensely shy but lack the kind of trust that close relationships are built on. Perhaps they were physically neglected or abused as children. Or, equally harmful, they may have experienced emotional rejection by their parents. Some of the most lonely people we have studied are those who were unsure about their parents' love. At times they felt their parents cared about them and accepted them. At other times their parents would ridicule them in front of others, tell them they'd never amount to anything, or act cold and angry at them for no apparent reason. This led to a building of emotional walls as a protection from uncertain love. They began to shield themselves from hurt by pulling back from close relationships. A basic feeling of distrust was established which makes them unable now to form intimate bonds. The result is a person who lives with intimacy at arm's length, lonely.

Rejection by peers is a trigger event for loneliness. Whether the loneliness will be long or short depends on the person's ability to earn acceptance from those rejecting him or from others. Terry felt intensely lonely when he was excluded by a group of friends for several weeks because he had broken up with a girl who was one of their best friends. Lou felt lonely on Friday afternoons when he and the other guys at the shop got paid. They'd always go to the bar and drink. He didn't like to drink, and they started calling him "Holy Joe." They even avoided him at lunch time; no one wanted to eat with him.

Many people feel lonely because they've lost close friends due to moves. Even though they may write occasionally and even visit once in a while, it's no longer the same. The closeness, spontaneity, and day to day contact are usually gone. For the person moving, there is the dual burden of losing past friends and not having new ones to immediately fill the void. The first one or two years after a move are often very lonely times. Marie found she became very lonely when her family moved from California to Virginia. In California she had several very close friends. She was never really able to make new friends in Virginia. She became sick a lot and was pretty much a loner during her last two years of high school. After finishing high school, she moved back to California and found an apartment with three of her old friends.

A sizable number of people feel lonely because they don't have anyone to talk with about the things that are important to them. They feel that people either don't really care how they feel or don't understand. This is true both for singles and for married people. Joan, a twenty-one-year-old university student, described her loneliest experience: "I felt that I couldn't tell my closest friends about a personal matter. I really needed to tell someone, but I felt they wouldn't understand. I told them and they really didn't understand, but they tried to." Ann, a thirty-two-year-old divorcee, said, "I couldn't stand it anymore. He never listened to what I said. He always had something more important to do. I felt like a shell, like it didn't even matter if I was there. I had no one that I could share what I felt with. I felt all alone."

Death of a loved one ushers in loneliness for virtually everyone. After the shock and the grief comes the loneliness, the missing and longing. The permanence of the separation and the irreplaceable spot that a father, mother, child, close relative, or friend had may create an emptiness that lingers for a lifetime. Even when the worst of the pain is gone and new relationships are built, the moments of emptiness may still appear. Frank's mother died when he was twelve years old. As he put it, ''I have always felt as if someone needlessly took her from me and my family. I have always felt somewhat depressed because of this occurrence. There always seems to be a void in my life, because she meant so much to me. She will never be replaced. She was the only person who really could understand me. I never felt lonely until she died.''

Alienation from God, being a leader, dating break-ups, divorce, being a stranger in a new country, sickness, having problems with parents, and temporary physical separation are some of the many other triggering events of loneliness we'll discuss in following chapters.

The feeling of being cut off from those who are emotionally significant is common to all these experiences of loneliness. To feel lonely is to feel disconnected. For those who have difficulty starting a close relationship, it is felt as the *lack* of being wanted and belonging. For others, loneliness is due to the *loss* of an intimate relationship through physical or psychological separation. In either case, we feel isolated and unable to cross a gap that we want desperately to cross. Loneliness is an indication of need. It tells us that our interpersonal system is out of kilter. Loneliness is due to a deficiency of intimacy. Not everyone has the same amount of need for intimate and affirming relationships. Some people need lots of close friends. Others seem to get along fine with memories or pets. But all human beings have *some* level of need for intimacy.

Human intimacy is simply a sense of togetherness with another person. It is a relationship in which we can give and receive of each other's deepest feelings and be accepted and understood.

Intimacy is being able to talk, laugh, and weep with another without fear of rejection. It's feeling we belong. Intimacy is to feel needed. When we are cut off due to defects in our personalities, conflicts in our relationships, situations, or roles that we assume, we feel lonely.

Loneliness is not the same as alone-ness. Loneliness is *feeling* alone, not being alone. Loneliness is more directly related to how *satisfied* we are with our relationships than to how often we have social contacts or to how many friends we have. Hermits may be happy, because they aren't looking for a large input of intimacy. It may well be that hermits are basically shy people who find loneliness less frightening than people.

Though we sometimes feel lonely when we're by ourselves, we also actively seek times apart from people. Indeed, a sizable percentage of people actually choose to be by themselves to think as a response to loneliness. In general, our attitudes toward being alone are taught. Our society considers it more normal to walk down the street with a portable radio blaring in our ears, or to have the television on when we're home alone (even though we're not watching it), than to value solitude. It used to be that solitude was desired, not avoided. Most of us are likely to experience loneliness in the midst of silence and aloneness, simply because we're taught to avoid facing ourselves in such situations.

At the same time, people may be lonely when they're in large crowds. Have you ever been in a group where you didn't know anyone, but everyone else seemed to be acquainted? How did you feel? Chances are you felt momentarily lonely and had a strong urge to somehow break into the inner circle. If you were socially skilled, you probably began striking up conversations with others, and the panic of loneliness slowly disappeared. Being physically alone or being with others is not directly related to loneliness, then.

Different Kinds of Loneliness?
Psychologists still aren't sure whether there is only one expe-

rience of loneliness or several different kinds. We know that there are different surface causes of loneliness. We also know that there are different intensities. The wider the gap between what we desire in our relationships and the intimacy we actually experience, the more lonely we'll feel. Singleness may be either an excruciatingly lonely experience or a time for creative living. This largely depends on the level of expectations one has. Similarly, the loss of an especially intimate relationship will be felt more keenly than the loss of one that has not penetrated into our emotions so deeply or for so long.

M.I.T. psychologist Robert Weiss has suggested that there are two kinds of loneliness.[7] He calls the first *emotional isolation*. This is due to the lack of a deep and emotionally satisfying relationship with another person with whom we share ourselves. This is usually found in a husband-wife relationship, for example. Weiss also suggests that we feel lonely when we are socially cut off. He calls this *social isolation*, or the absence of an emotionally satisfying network of friends. We do not fully share ourselves with people in our network, but to belong to and be valued by several other people beyond our families or a close friend seems important. Loneliness results when we are somehow cut off from either kind of relationship.

2

WHAT DIFFERENCE DOES IT MAKE?

Kevin Anderson made a gallant attempt to become the youngest person to swim the English Channel in June 1978. After seven and a half hours of swimming, eleven-year-old Kevin was taken from the water just six miles from the French coast. The Channel Swimming Association said that one of his major problems was loneliness.

From the air it looked like the aftermath of a giant celebration, with bits of colored paper dotting the landscape.[1] It was actually the scene of mass suicide. Over 900 men, women, and children had become victims of a deep need to belong, to be part of a paradise on earth. "Father" Jones lay on the steps to his podium-throne, where he had ruled over his "family" and exhorted their mass suicide. Many were considered rejects by society; People's Temple offered them a home. They were looking for affirmation and acceptance. In the end, however, they were victims of their "father's" paranoia. But they died together — belonging.

There are approximately thirteen hundred religious groups, or cults, in the United States today.[2] They are a symbol of the rootlessness, the deep inner need to feel connected and to belong, which marks much of American life today. Many of the converts to cults are young people. Many of them have weak family ties. Most of them are searching for personal meaning for their lives.

Loneliness makes a difference. We feel, think, and act differently when we're lonely. For some of us there is only a small difference. Loneliness isn't always intense — it may just be a nagging discomfort — nor does it often last long. For others of us, however, loneliness colors our whole existence. We see people and life differently. We do things we would otherwise never think of.

In this chapter, we'll examine how people feel when they're lonely, the physical problems caused by loneliness, what lonely people do, how they think, and how loneliness is related to spiritual well-being. Many of our comments will be about the long-term or chronically lonely, but most of them also apply in less intense or prolonged form to the short-term lonely as well.

How Does Being Lonely Feel?

About 52 percent of the several hundred people that we have questioned say that they sometimes or often feel empty when they're lonely. "Being lonely feels empty and hollow, like a single barren tree in the dead of winter," according to Lynn, a twenty-one-year-old college student. Another wrote, "It's an emptiness inside my body, like a hollow tube, and my head was often empty of thoughts."

For many, then, loneliness is feeling that they are missing something, or more correctly, some*one*, in their lives. In the process of being without a desired close relationship, they feel they've lost part of themselves. For Rick, it felt "as if someone had cut part of my body, or my life, away." They feel a deep inner void and have no sense of purpose in life. The absence of a vital connection with someone who cares leaves them feeling like a shell. As Tom put it, "Loneliness is a very empty, wholly deserted feeling. You want to reach out for love and a lover, but there is none there." Without intimacy, there's emptiness. Loneliness is an unfulfilled desire for companionship.

Closely related to emptiness is a feeling of being *isolated*. Almost 64 percent of the people we surveyed said they felt cut off, alone, and separated from those who are emotionally important to them. "It's like being left out in the middle of a desert by yourself," said one woman. George described his loneliness as feeling as if "I really don't have any friends. I always feel left out. It seems as though I'll never meet people and talk to them. It's a very dark and cold feeling."

Feeling isolated is normally the result of losing physical, psychological, or spiritual contact with those important to us. Among older, retired people, the break in companionship which produces feelings of isolation is often due to physical factors. Mildred is an eighty-year-old widow who has lived in the same home for fifty years. She lives in the country, about a half mile from her nearest neighbor and five miles from her oldest son. She is unable to drive due to failing eyesight, and there are no buses. She finds it difficult to walk. The only times she has a chance to talk with anyone are when her son and his family drop by two or three times a week, or a neighbor or church friend drops by. She has been feeling increasingly lonely since her husband of fifty years died about four months ago. Mildred has been cut off from the intimate emotional companionship of many years with her husband. But she also has to contend with the physical facts of her life which isolate her from others.

For others of us, isolation is due to a break in relationships. About 48 percent of the people we investigated felt rejected when they were lonely, and 51 percent regularly felt they were misunderstood. Isolation is directly related to these feelings. In the case of rejection, we feel that someone we value doesn't want to relate to us, devalues us, and wishes we weren't around. That's a very lonely feeling. In the case of being misunderstood, loneliness is not due to being actively cut off. Rather, being misunderstood makes us feel like an emotional island, with no bridges between us and those who count in our lives; the connections are gone. Rejection and misunderstanding cause us to feel worthless. Feeling isolated and worthless is depressing. Lois is a sixteen-year-old who isn't dating, though her friends are. She feels intensely lonely: ''I feel detached and isolated. I also feel depressed and not worth anything to others.''

Depression is the most common feeling associated with loneliness. Eighty-one percent of the people we've interviewed say that they are sometimes or often depressed when they're lonely. Depression rivals schizophrenia as the top mental health problem in America. Up to 15 percent of the general population suffers from depression at any given time; as many as 70 percent of college freshmen fight bouts of depression.

There seem to be several common causes of depression. Each is closely related to loneliness as well.

We don't realize the seriousness of the connection between loneliness and depression until we look at suicide statistics. About one of every 200 people affected by severe depression commits suicide. There are 50,000 to 70,000 suicides annually in the United States. Between 1964-74 the suicide rate for children between the ages of five and fourteen doubled. Severe depression in children is becoming more chronic and widespread. One can only wonder about the relationship between child suicides and the accelerating divorce rate. Suicide is now the second leading cause of death for young people between the ages of fifteen and twenty-four. Approximately 80,000 young people in this age category try it each year — about 4,000 of them succeed.

Certainly loneliness is not the only cause of suicide. But the emptiness, depression, purposelessness, and isolation that so many of us feel when we're lonely may tip the scales for the intensely lonely. In the midst of bitterness over ended relationships, feelings of social failure, and depression, the most lonely people sometimes try to escape through the one door they feel they can control — death.

Depression often comes when we fail to meet the expectations that we or others have of us. The gap between what we'd like and the way things are can easily cause depression. The same is true for loneliness. We have consistently found that people with the lowest feelings of self-worth are the depressed and lonely. At this point we're not sure whether low self-worth or loneliness comes first. Probably either can and does trigger the other. Some people feel worthless because they're unable to form or keep close relationships. Psychologists suggest that loneliness comes when our circle of close friends is smaller or less satisfying than we desire.[3] The reason that many single women in their late twenties feel lonely and depressed is, in part, the expectations they've been taught to have. That is, women who are worth much in our society are supposed to "be caught" by the time they're twenty-five. When they turn thirty without being snared, they not only feel the pressure of friends and family who wonder why, but they also feel the urgency, despair, and loneliness of not meeting their own desires.

Another reason for depression is the *disruption of attachments* that we have. Very early in life we form emotional bonds with those who care for us. These bonds, usually with parents — as well as those we later form with close friends, a spouse, and our own children — are essential for us to physically and psychologically survive. We don't give up our relationships without pain. For example, one study of over four thousand widowers found that they had a significantly higher death rate for the first year of being unattached than did others of the same age who had not experienced such loss. People who experience more loss and separation are more likely to be depressed.[4] The loneliness of loss is not restricted to spouses. For example, there is evidence that the most stressful life event and best predictor of emotional or physical illness is the loss of one's child.

We'll consider some fascinating relationships between loneliness and disease a bit later in this chapter.

It is apparent, then, that disruption of close relationships not only promotes depression but triggers intense loneliness. We are made to love and be loved. Close relationships are vital not only with humans but with God as well. King David experienced both depression and loneliness when his sin cut off his communion and intimacy with God (Psalm 38).

Depression also seems to occur when we *feel helpless*.[5] Most bouts of depression are set off by some external, unpredicted event over which we have little or no control. Depressed people tend to have a pessimistic view of their own abilities. They not only feel helpless, but they also feel hopeless. They're set to interpret their responses as failures and are especially sensitive to possible obstacles. We can understand, then, how shy people get locked into loneliness and depression. They may want friends but feel they aren't able to make friends. They often think up multiple excuses for why they don't try to form friendships. The fact that the poor typically show up as more lonely may also be related to learned helplessness. They have typically been taught that they do not have the resources to control the events of living. Their lives are so filled with unsolvable daily problems that they learn that what they do really doesn't affect what happens very much. Poor people have been found to experience twice as many stressful events as those in the highest income groups, and to have the fewest human helping resources available.[6]

Loneliness and helplessness are also related.[7] The greater the sense of helplessness we have over the creation or loss of close relationships, the more lonely we are likely to be. Elderly patients in a nursing room who were allowed to choose when their visitors would come were much less lonely than those who had only unpredictable "drop ins."[8] In general, elderly people feel as though they can do little to change their lonely condition. One study which discovered that 90 percent of the elderly people surveyed felt they were more lonely than they had been when younger, also found that about 50 percent felt nothing could be done to change their loneliness.[9] Younger widows are also more likely to actively seek new relationships than older widows.[10] Dating partners who want a relationship to end and see themselves as the one initiating the break-up feel less lonely and depressed.[11] Loneliness is less likely to be passive and depressive if we see ourselves as the cause of the loneliness due to some factor (like lack of effort) which we can control.

Although depression seems to go along with loneliness, peo-

ple can be lonely without being depressed.[12] People who are
depressed when lonely are more anxious and angry. They are
also less satisfied with the nonsocial areas of their lives; life in
general is much bleaker and pessimistic for the depressed-
lonely.

Loneliness carries with it a desire for things to be different.
There is frequently an underlying sense of yearning and searching
for a person who can plug our emptiness and lift our spirits.
Often when we're lonely we are afraid that things won't change,
that the special someone won't be found, that others won't find
us worthwhile and include us. Over 50 percent of our interviewees
felt these kinds of anxieties when they were lonely. The inability
to make things different often results in anger and hostility.
People who are chronically lonely also seem to have greater
levels of hostility. While this may be understandable, it doesn't
help their cause much. Others pick up those feelings of hostility.
They hesitate to develop intimate relationships for fear of getting
emotionally hurt.

Are Lonely People Less Healthy?

Psychologist James Lynch has done an exhaustive analysis of
the connections between loneliness and death.[13] Although living alone is not necessarily the same as being lonely and his
findings are largely correlational, Lynch makes a powerful case
for the link between intimate companionship and health.

Almost 1 million people die each year from heart disease.
This amounts to about 55 percent of all deaths reported in the
United States. Heart disease is the leading cause of death for
American adults between twenty-four and sixty-five. In addi-
tion, heart disease disables a higher number of people in our
country than any other disease.

These facts have led many medical researchers to investigate
the possible causes of cardiovascular disease. Until recently,
however, most ignored the impact that human relationships
might have. Do broken relationships, bereavement, and loneliness have something to do with premature death?

The answer seems to be yes. Virtually without exception, unmarried people die earlier than married people. The death rate from heart disease is 2 to 5 times higher for nonmarried people. Nonmarrieds include divorced, widowed, and other single persons. For both sexes and all races, the single and divorced die early. For *all* major causes of death, divorced males have a death rate 2 to 6 times higher than their married counterparts. Almost every kind of cancer happens at a significantly higher rate for nonmarrieds. Even death rates from motor vehicle accidents are 4 times greater for nonmarrieds, and cirrhosis of the liver is 7 times higher. Six of the eight top causes of death are clearly linked with companionship and loneliness. Married people have 50 percent fewer chronic health problems which can be considered disabling; they seem to have better ability to cope. In almost every kind of health-related institution, the percentage of nonmarried patients is much higher than the percentage of nonmarrieds in the general population.

Married people who are emotionally isolated from their spouses and unhappy are a bit better off than unmarrieds, but not much. Married men who feel a lack of emotional support from their wives or who neglect their wives and children in favor of work report a greater number of mental problems and develop heart disease much more frequently than happily married men.

The emotional trauma of losing a loved one also takes its toll. People who experience such a loss have a high death rate during the first year of attempted adjustment.[14] Rates for the bereaved average 40 to 50 percent higher during that time than for others of the same age group.[15] About three-quarters of these deaths are due to heart disorders. Indeed, these people seem to die of broken hearts! Suicide rates are also two-and-a-half times higher for the newly widowed in the first year after their spouse's death than for intact couples.

The typical nonmarried person stays in the hospital longer for identical problems than marrieds; they also visit physicians more frequently. It seems likely that they unconsciously are searching for a human concern that they otherwise would not receive. As many insightful doctors will admit, a large percentage of people who visit them seem to do so more out of a need for attention, and for a few moments of intimate sharing, than for medically significant problems.

Perhaps the most common physical experience that's connected with loneliness is fatigue. Loneliness drains our physical energy and robs us of the ability to initiate relationships. This is especially true when a very close relationship has been lost. If we have also given up hope for renewing or replacing the intimate, we'll find ourselves physically sapped. Every move may take all the energy we have.

Facing life without the desired companion is often so painful that sleeping may seem to be the only solution. It's not unusual to find intensely lonely people sleeping nine or ten hours a night. More often than not, they'll still complain about being tired and not getting enough rest.

One further expression of loneliness centers in the stomach and viscera. Associated with the emotion of emptiness, many people have an empty feeling in the pit of their stomach. One young woman, who moved away from her parents' home and family of ten to live alone, says that at times she feels as if ''a hole is being gnawed through my stomach.'' Often there is the feeling of stomach upset and diarrhea-like queasiness.

We've also found that people with negative self-esteem are more likely to feel faint and bored, short of breath, tired, and tight in the chest when they're lonely. These physical feelings are symptoms of anxiety. People who doubt themselves have a hard time feeling hopeful that their loneliness will end. They are sensitively tuned to negative cues from others; they pick up indications of rejection quickly. All this emotional turmoil is then expressed physically.

What Do People Do When They're Lonely?

Up to this point, we've been looking at how people feel when they're lonely. Now we'll turn our attention to what they *do*. In order to answer this question, we asked people to tell us how likely it was that they generally did each of twenty-three different things when they were lonely.

Surprisingly, the top two responses did not involve other people. Over 67 percent said they were most likely to listen to music. Almost 66 percent said they were most likely to get alone and think. Both of these actions seem to express the need for *reflective solitude*. From earliest biblical times, music has spoken to the human spirit. It has the capacity to agitate, excite, and disorder as well as the power to quiet and make us feel melancholy. Most often we turn to quiet and nostalgic music when we're lonely. Music excites the imagination and intensifies the emotions. It can lift us or encourage us to wallow in self-pity. It can be a vehicle for the release of our deepest feelings, allowing us to get a constructive handle on the direction our lives should take. But it can also incapacitate us with the memories of unfulfilled dreams. Music that reaches into our hearts and gives us hope is a valuable tool in helping us cope with loneliness. Christian songs that are realistic in their lyrics but counter momentary despair with the comforting, caring, and intimate presence of God in both lyric and music are vital. If the lyrics focus only on human hurts and tragedy, they will depress us further. If they focus only on God's greatness and power but don't connect with human need, they'll feel cold and distant. Melody, harmony, and rhythm that correspond to the lyrics can take us from feelings of loneliness and helplessness to feelings of God's loving presence and hopefulness.

Fortunately, when our needs for intimacy aren't being met, most of us don't rush out and grab on to somebody for a security blanket — that's a sure way to disaster. Most of us resist ping-pong relationships. Rather, we first try to put the pieces together and gain new resolve for the future. This is a healthy response to loneliness, in its initial stage. It helps us to bring order out of emotional chaos. We need to guard against letting ourselves slip into a continuing pattern of social withdrawal, however. Focusing on our hurts or our inadequacies can paralyze us. Once we have some sense of our bearings, we need to actively tear away from self-focus and reach out to others. If we allow ourselves to continue mulling, we'll only find ourselves becoming more depressed and less able to act constructively.

The best way to guard against excessive reflective solitude is to include God in our experience. As we express our feelings to Him in prayer and immerse ourselves in portions of Scripture which parallel our situation, we may find considerable relief. Religiously oriented responses are made by a sizable proportion of people. About 39 percent of the people we surveyed pray when lonely, and 24 percent read the Bible. Given the fact that over 50 percent of them identified themselves as "Christian," however, it's instructive that so few turn to God at a time of deep personal need.

A large number of people do try to make *contact with close friends* when they're lonely. They search out friends to talk with about their feelings (54 percent), spend time with a close friend just to be together (51 percent), go someplace where their friends will be (40 percent). Friends help us to feel wanted. They help us to clarify our feelings. They're a source of comfort. They may give us helpful suggestions. The loneliest people, of course, are those without friends who seem to understand and care. They're forced to seek relief from their loneliness in other, less directly helpful ways.

We found, for example, that a large percentage of people engage in *nonsocial diversion* such as eating (52 percent), studying/working (32 percent), or shopping (35 percent). While these activities may temporarily lessen feelings of loneliness, they are generally not effective in overcoming more intense and longer-term loneliness. In addition, they may have some bad side-effects. For example, many people who are lonely tend to overeat. Not only does this affect their health, but it may also affect their relationships. They may gain so much weight over a period of time that they become socially undesirable. This only worsens their loneliness.

This is not to say that diversionary activities aren't helpful.

They have the advantage of helping us to focus on things other than our feelings and failures. We need to be careful, however, to make sure our diversions do not become habits.

A smaller percentage of people are likely to engage in *searching responses* such as going to a dance, play, or movie, or taking a drive. By going to places where we will be with other people, we may hope to find a person who will meet our needs. Just being in a place with others may help. This depends in part on who else is there. For example, if people go to a dance and end up as wallflowers, their sense of isolation and loneliness may only be worsened. On the other hand, they may meet someone who will become a friend.

A small but important proportion of people try to cope with loneliness by engaging in *sensually oriented* responses. These include drinking and smoking, taking drugs, and becoming sexually involved with someone. While it is not suggested that the only reason people become alcoholics, drug users, or engaged in sexual relations is loneliness, there is evidence that loneliness plays an important role in this development.

Alcohol is a convenient escape hatch for many. Manufacturers prey on this. Alcohol and tobacco industries spend $1 million *each day* to sell their goods. Seven out of every ten billboards I drive by in the San Francisco Bay Area carry liquor or cigarette ads! Per capita alcohol consumption has risen steadily during the past thirty years, mirroring the accelerated break-up of marriage and family life and the resulting loneliness. There are an estimated 9 to 15 million alcoholics in the U.S. Another 6 million are considered prealcoholics. Over a million teens between the ages of twelve and seventeen have serious alcohol problems. About 9 percent of today's teens admit to being drunk at least once a week; the amount of alcohol drunk by juveniles averages forty ounces a week. The effects are devastating: more than half of heavy teen drinkers have stolen, more than a third have damaged property, half of all assaults occur while under the influence, and nearly eight thousand young people are killed in

auto accidents each year. What starts out as an attempt to dull the
pain of rejection and loneliness, or to prevent it by fitting in with
the crowd, ends up destroying.

Drug abuse has also been linked to loneliness.[16] For many it is
an attempt to escape the pain of an empty and lonely life, to
move beyond the world of crushing reality to a world of freedom. An estimated $2.5 billion is spent on legal drugs each
year; another $2 billion goes for illegal drugs. There are an
estimated 600,000 Americans hooked on heroin. Marijuana
sales are the third biggest business in the U.S.,[17] according to
the Department of Commerce. It ranks behind General Motors
and Exxon, but ahead of Mobil, IBM, and GE in sales volume.
Over 100 million *new* minor tranquilizer prescriptions are written in the U.S. each year to help people cope with anxiety and
stress. Cocaine has become a billion dollar a year enterprise. Its
use is concentrated primarily in the eighteen to thirty-five age
group, though it is becoming as popular as marijuana among
younger teens. One of the biggest factors influencing young
people to take drugs is social pressure. They're afraid that if they
don't conform they'll be cut off from their peers. The *fear of
loneliness* leads thousands into a hell worse than loneliness. The
drug abuser is ultimately the victim of his own fears. He lives in
a paranoid world of stealing, murder, mistrust, friendlessness,
and bondage.

Free-lance sexual relationships have become commonplace
in the U.S. Singles bars have been referred to as "meat markets"
where lonely men and women often try to meet and master their
loneliness by mating. But sex and intimacy are not equatable.
The kind of intimacy which prevents or overcomes loneliness
takes time. It isn't created in one-night stands or dependent upon
physical prowess. It is born and nurtured in the context of caring
for the whole person.

The continuing rash of teen pregnancies is a good measure of
our society's sexual confusion. About 250,000 unwed teens
under eighteen give birth each year; about 50 percent are under
fifteen and 40 percent are unmarried. Many young girls permit,

even encourage, sexual relations. They often feel that having a baby will result in marriage. More often it leads to being a single parent and to a series of promiscuous relationships as the search for intimacy proceeds without fulfillment.

Finally, delinquency has also been linked to loneliness.[18] In 1978, 50 percent of all violent crimes in the U.S. were committed by teens. Age fifteen is the peak age for violence, and the rate of violence by juveniles has tripled between 1960-75. School vandalism costs $600 million each year. There were over 70,000 assaults against teachers in 1978. Lonely teens are more likely to: associate with other failing and rejected teens; engage in more vandalism, theft, and gambling; tend toward unconventionality and normlessness. They run away more and are more susceptible to peer pressure to use drugs and alcohol. One fourteen-year-old boy who had been unable to cope with either parents or school estimated that "eighty percent of being a delinquent is being lonely." A high percentage of delinquents come from broken homes. Though their outward behavior may camouflage their real feelings, they usually have deep needs for love and acceptance. Many have been shuttled from foster home to foster home during childhood. Their search to belong, combined with the sense of parental rejection they feel, frequently leads to involvement with others like them. Gangs form. Together, their delinquency becomes an expression of belonging and rejection against a world that has rejected them.

Does Loneliness Affect Social Interaction?

Do we relate to others in the same way when we're lonely as when we're not? The answer seems to be no. When we are lonely, we tend to make more statements about ourselves and ask fewer questions of our partners.[19] When we're lonely, we become caught up in the turmoil of our interior feelings and find it difficult to show interest in what others think and feel. Combined with this is a tendency to respond more slowly to the statements of others and become more brief and sparse in our own conversation. Obviously, this kind of interaction makes it tough to get or keep others interested in us. When people reach out, they expect a return on their investment. People will shy away from us if we are typically and tenaciously self-centered. Our feelings of loneliness will intensify and cause us to become even more preoccupied with our pain — a vicious cycle.

When we're intensely lonely, we often cling too tightly to others. We may be so desperate that we latch on to anyone who shows the slightest bit of interest in us. We may also make unusual and impossible demands on our family or friends. People don't like being hugged by a boa constrictor! When we're lonely we may want to be with a friend almost all of the time, call several times a day, and so forth. All of this has the same effect as garlic — it drives people away. In our loneliness, when we feel most isolated, we have a natural desire to feel attached, connected, united with someone. We must be careful, though, not to *demand* attachment, or we'll drive away the very people we need to uphold us.

One of the basic ways that we feel attachment is through the give and take of words. Words are bridges between people. They reach from one psyche to another. Given a chance, people tend to talk more when they're lonely. For example, people who are without a companion and live alone characteristically carry on extensive monologues with those who visit them. They have a deep need to be heard. Indeed, they have a deep need to hear themselves talking! It's as though talking assures them that they are still alive.

Chronically lonely people also tend to indiscriminately disclose more about themselves. They seem to need a target toward which to aim their intimate feelings. This often causes their "targets" to become uneasy and anxious; social rules tell them that such disclosure requires a deeper level of intimacy.

Doris talks all the time — about herself. She's one of those people who forces you to be socially honest. You don't dare ask "How are you?" unless you want to know all the gory details. Her answer could easily take an hour. She seems to talk without taking a breath, so there's no natural place to interrupt and limit the barrage. Doris has endless lists of things currently wrong with her and her life situation. She talks freely about very personal physical problems and openly reveals her past with a violent husband and abusive parents. She shares these intimacies with almost anyone who asks the fatal question "How are you?" The result is that people avoid her, and she is lonelier than ever.

Typically, chronic loneliness is associated with inadequate social skills. Those who are chronically lonely feel they are less effective in getting their way with other people. Some research suggests they are actually more manipulative and coercive than the nonlonely.[20] That is, they have not acquired the more subtle graces of persuasion and influence that allow them a measure of control over their social world without driving people away from them. Lonely people, perhaps because of shyness and poor social abilities, are less willing to take relational risks. While this may first start out as temporary withdrawal, it may soon become a way of life — a permanent escape.

How Do Lonely People Think?

When we're lonely, it's awfully hard to think positively. This is another chicken or egg first issue. Loneliness seems to foster pessimism, and pessimism encourages loneliness. Lonely people have a more negative view of human nature in general. They're also more negative about specific people — that is, chronically lonely people are less accepting of others, have less trust, and believe less in a just world. One of the obvious results is that it's tough to initiate relationships when we feel that way about others. There is an underlying fear of others that may even cause active avoidance of them.

We've already noted the clear relationship between pessimism, helplessness, and depression. It appears that less-lonely and temporarily lonely people are likely to focus on the immediate and the near future, which they can have some effect on, while the chronically lonely focus on the more distant future, about which they can do little.[21] Because of their sense of helplessness, the chronically lonely are more pessimistic about themselves and their future. They get caught in a mire of defeatist thinking which paralyzes their ability to do something constructive about their loneliness. The profound wisdom of Philippians 4:8 can be partially glimpsed as we see the extent to which our thinking affects our feelings. We would do well to think thoroughly about "whatever is true, whatever is honorable, whatever is pure, whatever is lovely, whatever is of good repute, if there is any excellence and if anything is worthy of praise." Loneliness feeds upon pessimism; optimism, however difficult to develop, fosters the ability to initiate and maintain close relationships. Without hope there cannot be intimacy — only loneliness and despair. Intimacy requires belief in the good intentions and trustworthiness of one another. Optimism is very close to faith in that it looks and sees the impossible as possible; it expects good.

Lonely people also seem to have difficulty concentrating. Because concentration requires the harnessing and focusing of energy, loneliness militates against it. First, any concentrating we do tends to be on ourselves and our loneliness. Our experience is like being caught in quicksand; we easily find our thoughts totally trapped by our feelings of loneliness and self-pity when we're lonely. Second, loneliness reduces our supply of creative energy. We feel drained and are unable to generate enthusiasm for anything outside our small, constrictive sphere. The practical implications of this aren't too difficult to imagine. Intense loneliness is associated with school failure and interferes with work performance that requires substantial problem-solving or precision. The reduction and diffusion of energy that marks intense or prolonged loneliness affects our overall sense of purpose and direction.

Does Loneliness Make A Spiritual Difference?

My colleague, Ray Paloutzian, and I have developed a twenty-item Spiritual Well-Being Scale to measure both existential and religious well-being experiences.[22] Our study of the relationships between loneliness and spiritual well-being has revealed this consistent picture: People who are lonely feel life has little satisfaction or purpose. To a smaller degree, they also report less, positive experiences with God. They report less satisfaction in private prayer than the nonlonely and have more difficulty believing God is personally concerned about their daily problems. They have trouble believing that God accepts them for who they are, and they experience God as more judgmental than do the nonlonely. Their relationship with God does not help them cope with their loneliness.

Our current studies only tell us that high loneliness and low spiritual well-being go together. It is possible, of course, that a breakdown in one's relationship with God produces loneliness. Loneliness not only lowers our sense of well-being, but negative feelings and isolation from God promote loneliness on the deepest levels. It is this sense of meaninglessness and aloneness that has led such atheistic thinkers as Camus and Sartre into utter despair and loneliness. This kind of loneliness can only be overcome by being reconciled to God through Jesus Christ. The breaking of our most fundamental relationship — the one with God — leads to a sense of emptiness and lifetimes of searching for some way to satisfy the need for God. But the loneliness of existence apart from God can only be met by restoration. His indwelling presence can turn the emptiness to fullness.

3

THE ROOTS OF
LONELINESS

It wasn't always this way. There was a time when loneliness was unknown, a stranger to human experience. The ache
and anguish of separation were once alien emotions. The
searching and longing for completion were foreign. What
happened? Why has loneliness become a frequent and frightening
companion in lives?

A proper understanding of the origins and nature of loneliness
begins with the biblical account of the creation: "Then God
said, 'Let *us* make man in *our* image, in *our* likeness'" (Genesis
1:26).[1] While Scripture makes it clear that there is only *one*
God, the words "us" and "our" suggest the plurality of His
being. As surely as God is one, He is a Trinity. God is a social
being. From before the beginning, the Father, Son, and Spirit
fellowshipped with each other. God created man to have additional companionship, to have those with whom He could express
His overflowing and infinite love. God walked in the garden and
sought the fellowship of Adam and Eve.

Human beings, made in the image of God, are *fundamentally*
social beings. Our need for God and other people is not derived
from pleasurable associations of being fed and being held when
we were infants, as modern psychologists have argued. Rather, it

derives from our being made in God's likeness. We are made to love and be loved.

Further evidence of this is found in Genesis 2:18: "The Lord God said, 'It is not good for man to be alone. I will make a helper suitable for him.'" While man was made to have communion with God, he was created a finite being who could never have total communion with the Creator. So God created Eve, a companion who would complement Adam. Adam and Eve were made in God's image and reflected the communing, intimate relationship of God. It's uncertain whether Adam felt loneliness up to the point that God created Eve. But God knew he had a need that required an intimate relationship, because man had been created to love. And love requires expression.

The Loneliness of Sin

Unfortunately, the beautiful picture was marred and broken forever. Misunderstanding and blame replaced the intimacy God had intended. Adam and Eve soon found themselves irreversibly separated from God and from each other. The serpent, by appealing to pride and power, broke the most intimate relationship that could ever be known. The result was humiliation, hiding, and hurt. Adam and Eve gained knowledge but lost the intimacy of unbroken love.

The hideousness of sin was that it broke communion. By reaching for power, man lost his footing and fell from love. It was not that God ceased to love. Rather, because absolute love requires absolute integrity, Adam and Eve could no longer *receive* God's love as before. Neither could they give love to God or each other as before. In order to love and be loved there must be honesty — a willingness to become and remain vulnerable. Love also requires a focus on our companion rather than upon ourselves. At the realization of sin, Adam and Eve hid. Their attention shifted from God's beauty to their shame. Instead of being only able to know God and His love, they now knew themselves and their corruption. They became self-centered, fascinated, and frightened by what they saw. They tried to hide despite knowing that God was fully aware of their wrongdoing. Their sin isolated them from their Creator. Intimacy was crushed because integrity was lost.

With the emergence of sin came a total distortion of human character and relationships. Romans 3:10-18 graphically describes how our understanding, motivation, self-worth, behavior, speech, emotions, and moral character have all been warped by sin. Virtually all the works of the flesh listed in Galatians 5:19-21 refer to acts which divide human beings from each other and also separate them from God. Sin opposes love. It casts us, self-centered, into the pit of loneliness and isolation.

In their new individualism, Adam and Eve blamed. It was the original "pass the buck" act. They tried to look good by denying who they were, by placing the responsibility for their sin on others. Somehow they felt that they could convince God and themselves that they were still okay and that nothing had changed within them. In truth, blaming is deception; it tries to preserve a facade of perfection. It's an ineffective ego-defense mechanism we employ to mask the truth from ourselves and others. The price for maintaining ego-defenses is loneliness. When we can no longer allow ourselves to be known as we really are, because what we are is shameful, we are faced with a basic difficulty in bridging the gap between. We cannot understand ourselves, and we often feel misunderstood.

Because of their sin, Adam and Eve also lost their place of earthly security. They no longer belonged in the garden. God drove them out into a wilderness of risk and uncertainty. Ever since that time, human beings have continually searched for a place of belonging.

The awful isolation of sin is described in several other places in Scripture. David knew the agony of intense loneliness repeatedly through his life: In Psalm 25 he cried to the Lord, "Turn to me and be gracious to me, for I am lonely and afflicted. The troubles of my heart have multiplied; free me from my anguish. Look upon my affliction and my distress and take away all my sins'' (vv. 16-18). The psalmist describes his feelings of isolation in Psalm 88: ''I am set apart with the dead, like the slain who live in the grave, whom you remember no more, who are cut off from your care. You have put me in the lowest pit, in the darkest depths.... You have taken from me my closest friends and have made me repulsive to them. I am confined and cannot escape; my eyes are dim with grief'' (vv. 5-6, 8-9).

Man cannot approach God with unconfessed sin — the scorching light of God's character burns a painful hole through his defenses. In order to cope, some try to maintain a relationship with a God-myth. They change God's character by downplaying His justice and emphasizing His all-accepting love. God, for some, is a never condemning granddaddy who simply affirms what they are and do. Unfortunately, such a God is not real and cannot fill the empty places of the spirit. Others have tried to cope with God by trying to get rid of Him altogether. They have even pronounced Him dead, as in the ''God is Dead'' theology of the mid-1960s. The irony, of course, is that in so doing they've not only pronounced the death of any relationship with God that would quench their lonely despair, but they've also pronounced their own deaths. Removing God has simply plunged them further into loneliness.

The guilt that sin brings also hinders human relationships. It brings self-condemnation and a corresponding reluctance to be open in relationships. We fear rejection: ''If people knew what I was really like, they wouldn't like me.'' Unresolved guilt prevents intimacy and promotes superficial relationships. Guilt-ridden people are bound up in self-focus and self-protection. They are not free to be known, so they lock off portions of themselves.

Some modern psychologists argue that the concepts of sin and guilt are the causes of emotional disorders, and we need to get rid of such harmful notions. The guilt of unconfessed sin is emotionally and interpersonally upsetting. However, instead of trying to remove guilt by saying there is no sin, we need to resolve guilt by repentance.

Perhaps the most terrible loneliness ever experienced due to the isolation of sin is recorded in the New Testament. *"My God, my God, why have you forsaken me?"* (Mark 15:34) expresses an anguish and an emptiness we will never know. Because He loved us, God turned His back on His only Son. At the moment when Jesus effected the redemption of man by taking upon His perfect Self the full judgment of God for human sin, He was totally alone. The eternal communion and perfect intimacy that had been from forever was broken. Christ experienced the pit of hell in order to bring about the possibility of a restored, intimate, and eternal relationsip between man and God.

In the end, those who reject this means of restoration will also be rejected. They will experience the full impact of isolation from God (Matthew 25:41-46). Hell is the place of absolute isolation and utter loneliness. A major part of hell's psychological agony will be the inability of those consigned there to experience love. They will be forced to face themselves without the shield of ego-defenses. They will be unable to love or be loved because God is the source of all love, and they will be cast from His presence. Completely separated from God, they will be unable to form and maintain intimate relationships. Without God there can be no love. Without love there is only separation and loneliness. The inner agony and emptiness of an eternity without love will be their only companion.

Sin also introduced death and made it the unavoidable finality of human experience (Genesis 3:22-23). For non-Christians death is a final and permanent separation. For all, it breaks deep attachments and leaves those who are left behind feeling abandoned. At the death of a loved one we lose the belonging, acceptance, and communion that were uniquely ours with that person. Our memories live, but they can't replace the new moments for sharing that life continues to bring. Consequently, death brings emptiness and loneliness. We know what was and can never recover it in the same way.

Death had a bitter sting prior to Christ's resurrection. Joseph's brothers pleaded with him to let Benjamin return because his loss and (in Jacob's eyes) probable death would mean the death of Jacob due to a broken heart. Job tore his robe and shaved his head upon learning of his children's sudden death. Naomi called herself Mara (bitterness) (Ruth 1:20) because of the bitterness and emptiness the deaths of her husband and two sons brought. Jesus himself wept at Lazarus' grave, prior to raising him. Even after Christ's victory over death, the departure of loved ones strikes deeply and leaves us feeling helpless and distressed. But it should not leave us hopeless. When a Christian dies there is the hope of reunion for Christian loved ones left behind — there is the anticipation of an eternity together.

The Loneliness of Servanthood

The fact that most people choose to cover up their corruption and try to find relief from loneliness apart from God puts those who attempt to follow God in a lonely position. The prophet Elijah came down with a mighty crash from his astounding victory over the prophets of Baal and the success of his prayers for rain. He sat by himself in a cave, feeling rejected and isolated. He knew no one who loved and followed his Lord (1 Kings 19:14). God recognized his need for assurance and revealed to him that there were seven thousand other faithful people in Israel. He was not alone.

Other Old Testament prophets also found themselves in Elijah's predicament. Jeremiah cried out, "O Lord, you deceived me, and I was deceived; you overpowered me and prevailed. I am ridiculed all day long; everyone mocks me. Whenever I speak, I cry out proclaiming violence and destruction. So the word of the Lord has brought me insult and reproach all day long" (Jeremiah 20:7-8).

David agonized:
I am a stranger to my brothers, an alien to my own mother's sons; for zeal for your house consumes me, and the insults of those who insult you fall on me. When I weep and fast I must

endure scorn; when I put on sackcloth, people make sport of
me. Those who sit at the gate mock me, and I am the song of
drunkards.... scorn has broken my heart and has left me
helpless; I looked for sympathy, but there was none, for
comforters, but I found none [Psalm 69:8-12, 20].

Because God's people will differ from those of the world in
the way they perceive and think, they will often find themselves
in lonely situations. This is especially true if they are whole-
hearted and single-minded in their commitment. Because fallen
man desires to make others in his own image, he seeks to be with
those who will complement him. Similarity affirms who we are
and the choices we make. When somebody comes along with
different ways of thinking or acting, we normally try to get them
to conform. If that fails we avoid them. Associating with those
who are different from us creates stress. Differences make us
wonder if we're right.

And that, humanly speaking, was why Christ was crucified.
Comparison with Him was threatening to those who didn't want
to change. The same is true with God's people. They will find
themselves rejected if they are too good, too truthful, too con-
scientious, or too candid about their beliefs. The way to belong
is to conform. Following the tune of a different drummer may
lead to a lonely march. That is why, of course, the practice of
Koinonia, or the community of the believers, is so crucial.

Apart from active rejection, however, the committed Christian who is lonely may feel that everyone else is going a different
way. The values and priorities of others may seem different, even
though they're also Christians. They may seem more concerned
with gadgets, comforts, and feathering their own nests than with
giving their time, talents, and energies for the cause of the Good
News. They may be overtly successful, while the committed
Christian tries to follow God conscientiously and isn't successful by the world's standards. The loneliness of following Christ
is especially painful when even other Christians don't seem to
understand or uphold your obedience. It leaves the servant of

God feeling all alone, unable to share because no one will understand.

James Johnson tells of a young man who, instead of taking a high paying job, chose to become a youth evangelist.[2] He was looked upon as irresponsible by his friends because he was not associated with an organization. They considered him to be an egomaniac who wasn't caring for his family. Both his friends and family saw him as weird and resented his attempts to serve the Lord. Though God was providing food, clothing, and shelter for them, the uncertainty of a regular income and the "foolishness" of following God's call set him apart from even the closest people in his life.

It's likely that Moses felt cut off also. His attempts to follow God's leading were met by constant grumbling by the Israelites. They threatened to kill him. Even his spokesman, Aaron, did not remain faithful. Moses stood virtually alone in his commitments among several hundred thousand people.

There are indications that Paul was lonely as he tried to stand for the Lord. He felt abandoned when "At my first defense, no one came to my support, but everyone deserted me" (2 Timothy 4:16a).

The picture isn't complete, however, until we realize that though following God's leading in our lives may often mean loneliness, it also gains us intimate communion with our heavenly Father. God's choicest servants — Elijah, Moses, Abraham, Paul, and others — have enjoyed the close and abiding presence of the Almighty. They were also given the companionship of several people who understood and stuck by them in the midst of trial.

Loneliness of Finitude

Not all loneliness is *directly* due to sin, though all loneliness can be ultimately traced back to the Fall of Adam and Eve from perfect relationship with God and each other. Loneliness is also due to our finiteness. We are not *omnipresent* beings — we can't be in more than one place at once. As a result, physical separation introduces loneliness. In several of his letters Paul intimated that he was lonely: ''Recalling your tears, I long to see you'' (2 Timothy 1:4*a*); ''I hope in the Lord Jesus to send Timothy to you soon, that I also may be cheered when I receive news about you. . . . And I am confident in the Lord that I myself will come soon'' (Philippians 2:19, 24).

One of the problems that many first-term missionaries face is loneliness. Usually we call it ''homesickness,'' as we do when kids go to camp or college for the first time. Homesickness is the desire to be with familiar faces in a familiar setting, but being unable to because of physical separation. It's none other than the longing of loneliness.

Likewise, we are not *omniscient*. We don't know everything. Though Satan's temptation of Eve implied that eating from the tree would allow her to escape finitude and know all, as God does, it didn't happen. Because we are not infinite in character, we can't know infinitely. As a result, not only do we distort what we do know (due to sin), but we are also unable to comprehend or understand everything.

This lack of knowledge brings loneliness into our lives in two ways. First, when things happen to us or our loved ones that we can't understand, we may feel as though God has abandoned us. We feel lonely because we are unable to stretch beyond the restraints of our limited knowledge. Our restricted understanding prevents us from sensing that God is there even when our finite minds fail to comprehend how. In the absence of complete knowledge we are thrown back to faith, which may also be weak. The result is a feeling of isolation from God. Second, our limited ability to know means that we will misunderstand and be misunderstood by other people. We cannot leap into each other's brains but are forced to relate and make decisions based on limited information. More often than we'd like to think, we misinterpret and stand isolated from each other as a result. Without understanding there is no bridge between individuals.

Misinterpretation, combined with the ego-defensiveness, frequently brings about judgment and further separation between people. When we judge another we elevate ourselves and place them in the painful position of feeling inferior. Normally we conclude that we are too good for them. And since we don't want to be dragged down to their level, we avoid or break off any close relationship with them. From the view of the judged, there is the pain of rejection that usually leads to attempts to escape from the relationship. Sometimes, of course, the misunderstandings are cleared up, confessions are made, and the relationship is restored. But there is always the remaining reflex of all self-preservation which makes intimacy a bit more difficult to achieve and maintain. Our emotions indelibly write the hurt of rejection into our spirits even when corrections are made.

The Loneliness of Doubt

Have you ever experienced doubts about your faith? There was a time in my life when I was plagued by them. The thoughts came even when I didn't want to think them: "Am I a Christian? Does God really exist? How can I know the Bible is true?" God began to feel distant and unreachable. I began to feel isolated and empty.

Doubt is simply a lack of certainty. There are a number of reasons why we experience it. The net effect is to plunge our relationship with God into chaos. Doubt breaks trust. It leaves us feeling alone and unable to turn to God. Doubt divides.

Satan is a polished doubt-thrower. One of his primary strategies for dividing God and man is to hurl doubts at us about God's *character* and intentions. Satan's very name means *Accuser*. The serpent questioned God's integrity in the garden: "Did God really say? You will *not* surely die" (Genesis 3:1,4). Satan questions God's *goodness*: "How can a just God allow such evil and brutality as a Nazi Germany and Amin's Uganda to exist? How could a God of love think of a place like hell and send people there?" Satan also questions God's *being*: "How do you know that God exists? Have you ever seen God? Isn't God just an extension of your longing for security? How can a spirit be a person?'' And so on. In our scientifically oriented culture these doubts are especially easy to stir up. Science focuses on the world of sight, touch, taste, feeling, and hearing. Anything that can't be physically measured is suspect or irrelevant. Satan is able to play successfully upon our fixation with the visible.

By planting doubts about God's existence and character, Satan turns us away from Him. Scripture says that ''anyone who comes to [God] must believe that He exists and that He rewards those who earnestly seek Him'' (Hebrews 11:6b). We can't enjoy the intimacy of knowing God if we don't believe He's there. If we doubt His being we won't seek Him, we won't find Him, and we'll never know Him. If we don't think on His good character and His loving intentions toward us, we'll draw back from a complete relationship with Him. *Our doubts will prevent us from giving ourselves to Him in complete faith and trust.*

Satan also capitalizes on our weaknesses to introduce doubts about God's love for us. If we harbor unconfessed sin in our lives, Satan takes advantage to further the division: ''How could God possibly love you after all you've done?'' ''There's no sense confessing anymore because God knows you don't really mean it.'' ''Why should He keep listening to your pleading? — you never change.'' Satan uses these helpless and hopeless feelings that come from failure to even introduce doubts about our redemption: ''How can you be a Christian when you do things like that?''

Doubts also enter in when prayers seem to be unanswered. Unanswered prayer may actually be prayer that has been answered ''no.'' Nevertheless, when we pray intensely and sincerely for something that we genuinely feel is God's will, and there is no apparent response, doubts may crowd in. We may decide to stop praying and take things into our own hands. Worse yet, we may become bitter and turn our hearts against God. David's anguish in Psalm 13 parallels that of many Christians: ''How long, O

Lord? Will you forget me forever? How long will you hide your face from me? How long must I wrestle with my thoughts and every day have sorrow in my heart? How long will my enemy triumph over me?'' (vv. 1-2).

Unfulfilled expectations may also cause doubts. When things don't turn out according to plan, our natural inclination is to feel discouraged. In some circles we have been taught that when we do things God's way we'll experience success — we'll get the exact job we wanted, the house we dreamed of, the praise we longed for, and the crowds we planned for. We only have to look as far as Jesus to know that this isn't necessarily true. By the world's standards He failed — only the lessons of history tell us differently. What happens if we give ourselves wholeheartedly to some purpose we feel God has called us to, only to experience failure? What happens when we genuinely try to please God in our actions, only to be taken advantage of and have our efforts bomb? When our expectations are inflated, doubts may crush us. God is more concerned with our character than our causes, with our person than our programs. Even when we understand this, Satan still tries to get us to doubt God by stirring up our natural discouragement.

The doubts of ''unanswered'' prayer and unfulfilled expectations most easily overwhelm those who don't take time to seek God. Satan is able to get his doubt darts lodged in our spirits more easily if we fail to pray, read His Word, and seek His ways throughout the day — every day. Many Christians try to run a spiritual Cadillac on a thimble of gas — they may spend only fifteen minutes a day praying and ''searching'' the Word. They don't consciously include God in daily decisions. It's no wonder that doubts overtake them. They simply don't have enough contact with God to be able to effectively combat their fears.

But suffering is the greatest point of testing. To the human mind it almost never makes sense. Our natural inclination is to ask: ''Why me? What did I do to deserve this? Why did God allow this?'' If we fail to consciously turn to God in our suffering and ask for grace to stand, we will begin to doubt His goodness. Suffering cuts against our sense of justice. Unless we accord God full sovereignty, we will begin to question His loving character. Satan challenged God's evaluation of Job's faith by asking for permission to make him suffer (Job 1:10-11). He felt that Job would be driven away from God if he suffered enough. Instead Job was faithful, though he had moments of doubt, and he drew closer to God as a result of his suffering. Even John, the outspoken and dogmatic herald of the Savior, experienced pangs of doubt and loneliness in his prison cell. The one who announced the coming of His Messiah sent messengers to ask, ''Are you the one who was to come, or should we expect someone else?'' (Luke 7:20). Apparently Christ's answer calmed John's doubts, and he died a triumphant death that united him with God forever.

Finally, doubting is sometimes a reflection of our development. Probably the teens and early twenties are the most doubt-filled times for most. There are at least two reasons for this. First, we're engaged in shaping our identity — choosing our beliefs, lifestyle, career, mate, and lifetime goals. Everything is up for grabs. Often this includes God.

Some people blame Christian colleges for causing a son or daughter's ''loss of faith.'' Most often such a turning from God is due to a series of personal choices, not to the college. However, for some who go to college (Christian or secular), broadened exposure to the thinking of others who are not Christians may create or aggravate doubts. This usually happens with those who have been sheltered from the thinking of non-Christians. Carefully guided exposure during high school, including opportunities for kids to think up rebuttals, is an important means of inoculation against later doubt. Doubt during teen years can, of course, be positive. Many young people in the throes of forming an identity turn from their past and are spiritually born again.[3]

Loneliness and Solitude
Scripture clearly distinguishes between being alone and being

lonely. Matthew 14:13-14, 23 and Luke 5:16 indicate that Jesus
sought out "lonely" places where He could pray and be alone.
After the stress of relating intimately to the needs of thousands,
He had to separate Himself. Though the places were "lonely"
(isolated, away from people), they met Jesus' need for solitude.

Throughout the years, the giants of the Christian faith have
sought places of solitude. For most it was a place of temporary
separation from people and intimate fellowship with God. Being
alone was not lonely because it was a time of renewal with the
Father. In the place of solitude, strength was found to minister to
the needs of others.

We live in a society in which solitude is generally avoided.
Stereos, radios, and TVs fill the silence with noise and distrac-
tion. This is probably due to the death of God in many lives.
When God isn't there, the emptiness and the self-confrontation
of solitude make being alone painful. Probably the most painful
psychological punishment devised is solitary confinement.
Though the agony of solitary is partially due to being there
against one's will for an unpredictable length of time, it is also
due to the absence of relationships with anyone, including God.
When God is there, there is fellowship that sustains, though not
without emotional scars even then.

Time alone with God is a vital part of the Christian's spiritual
and emotional well-being. Most often in Scripture this period of
meditation seems to have been at the start of the day. In our
society it would also do us well to seek a place of being alone in
the middle or at the end of the day. As we are drawn together with
God in the quiet times, we'll automatically find ourselves drawn
together with those around us, especially with others who love
the Lord.

4

IS CULTURE
THE CULPRIT?

The widespread experience of loneliness in modern America suggests that it is more than a personal pathology. It's a social problem of significant importance. If only a few people here and there were lonely, we could properly focus our attempts to understand on their unique situations. Because loneliness seems more like an epidemic than an exception, however, we need to broaden our outlook. Does our society provide common experiences and perspectives that promote loneliness? If so, attempts at remedy must take them into account. What things in our culture are making loneliness an American tradition? How do American educational, industrial, and media influences promote loneliness?

Four major revolutions have occurred in our society during the past 200 years. Each has fundamentally altered the ways we think about and act toward others. Each encourages loneliness, as the way of life it has ushered in soaks deeply into the fabric of American culture. We are all influenced to some extent by each of the revolutions. They are the *industrial*, *technological*, *ideological*, and *urban* revolutions.

I am not *totally* against the effects of these revolutions. Though we'll be emphasizing those things which have promoted alienation and loneliness, there are other — more positive — effects. I am not a nostalgic dreamer who prefers fly-covered outdoor rest stops to modern plumbing, or eighteen hour workdays to a forty hour week. Nevertheless, each revolution has had an ample supply of thorns to go with the roses. The thorns are subtle, though, because we don't usually notice them until they've caused infection.

People and Production

Imagine life prior to the industrial revolution. There were no large machines, no industries with ten thousand employees, no automobiles, no airplanes, and few large cities. Most of the population was rural and worked on farms to produce their food. Non-food stuffs were usually homemade, though with the emergence of crop surpluses some people began to use their extra resources to have a few items handmade by craftsmen. Craftsmen oversaw and participated in the production of their wares from beginning to end. Gradually, family businesses grew up. Families worked together in business much as they had in the fields. Even apprentices were treated like family members, living in and participating in non-business family life.

Contrast that picture with life after the industrial revolution began to transform America. The development of large-scale machines made highly skilled craftsmen less necessary. Goods could be mass produced much more efficiently and profitably. Tenement housing forced people into crowded, and often unclean, living situations. Families that once had room to move were now crowded together into a couple of small rooms. Employees were hired at the cheapest possible wages and expected to completely provide for themselves from those wages. Long hours in rather inhumane conditions were mandatory. The overriding goal became profit.

People began to be viewed as tools. They were expendable commodities in the drive for profit. Even today the worth of people is still measured in terms of cash. Somehow we feel that

the person earning fifty thousand dollars a year is more worthwhile *as a person* than someone earning five thousand a year.
Though it's untrue, we also begin to evaluate our own worth in
monetary terms. Furthermore, we normally form our relationships along commodity lines. We rarely choose those who seem
to be of a lower economic class to be our friends. While denying
that we have a class system, we regularly operate according to its
terms. It is important to note here that numerous studies have
found that loneliness increases as income decreases. Poverty
brings rejection and loneliness in a society which evaluates
people by their income.

The industrial system demands specialists. The heart of mass
production is the development of specialized functions, each of
which are reproduced many times by certain workers. We've all
seen pictures of the auto assembly lines, where this system has
worked *par excellence*. The system is just as widely used today
in white collar businesses (accounting firms, insurance companies, medical clinics). We are a nation of specialists. This makes
for greater preciseness of performance. But it also leads to at
least two not-so-positive effects.

First, we tend to approach people and problems from a narrow
point of view. As specialists, we are prone to fit people into our
frame of reference. The eye, ear, and throat specialist begins to
see eyes, ears, and throats rather than whole people. We begin to
dehumanize. That makes genuine interaction and the kind of
caring which promotes human intimacy virtually impossible.
Being treated as less than we are blocks the full sharing of who
we are and makes loneliness more probable.

Second, each specialization has its own foreign language.
Did you ever see a psychologist and a mechanical engineer try to
talk with each other? It doesn't take too long before they run out
of shared experiences and a shared language. To advance in our
chosen fields, we have to become immersed in specialized
language. The more we're immersed, the more difficult it is to
talk with those who aren't specialists with us. We may use the

same language, but in different ways. The focus of our lives is not the same; what matters to us may be very different from what matters to others. I'm a psychologist, so I feel free to pick on my own field. Psychologists are notorious for being unable to write in understandable English. They learn "psychologese" very well in order to be successful as professionals, but often find it difficult to communicate to nonpsychologists. If psychologists can't even talk to and understand each other, it's no surprise that loneliness seems to be increasing. Husbands and wives may not share the major portion of their lives (work!) because of a feeling that the other person can't understand — it's too technical. They become mentally isolated from one another.

Another effect of the industrial revolution was the development of bureaucracy in business and government. As organizations and population grew, clearly defined patterns of interaction also were formed. Bureaucracy treats people in terms of rules and roles. You've all met the lady at the motor vehicle bureau who could not possibly let you renew your license with a check because the rules said "cash only"? The bureaucrat not only defines the "customer" or "client" in role terms, but sees himself in the same way. Usually this is expressed in an attempt to ward off some appeal that is not covered by or goes outside the rules. The normal expression is, "I only work here." Bureaucracy treats people impersonally. Each person is seen as a representative of a larger group, not as an individual. Individuals are made for the rules, whether or not the rules fit. An act of kindness is seen as a violation of proper procedure and outside the bureaucrat's realm of authority. The ultimate effect, once again, is the feeling of being treated like a number. Because of the growth of bureaucracy, there is little sense of human compassion in much of today's organizational world. People treat other people in detached, carefully defined role-terms. It is rare to see genuine caring and intimacy because people normally show and know only very formal and limited things about each other. They don't get beyond the masks very easily. Unfortunately, this happens in churches as well as in government and business. Probably the most notable example is the way we treat pastors and missionaries.

One of the reasons for this breakdown in relationships is the enthroning of efficiency. Back when production and profit were not king and queen, there were no time clocks. People were not looked at suspiciously, like thieves, if they spent a few minutes talking with one another. Time was allowed for friendships.

In my profession of teaching, time is given according to need. No price tag is placed on it. I'll never forget the first time I experienced the efficiency view of time. I discovered that a person with whom I had been doing business kept track of every minute we spent on any phone call or office visit, and charged a hefty fee on top of the other costs. As you might guess, that didn't do much to further our personal relationship. From that point on it became "strictly" business, with very limited and *efficient* interaction!

The problem with a time-clock orientation to relationships is that it doesn't work. Relationships take time to develop. They aren't very efficient. In fact, making and keeping close relationships may have an adverse effect in terms of maximizing profits. But they will pay off with intimacy rather than loneliness. When we view people in efficiency terms, fitting them into a preplanned and carefully calculated portion of our lives, we cut off the possibility of intimacy. When we treat people like machines, we have to expect loneliness.

Finally, the industrial revolution has made a society of consumerism possible. We have graduated from subsistence to sales. Commercials greet us every seven minutes on television, billboards beckon, and newspapers advertise. We have learned to value the new and discard the old. Obsolescence is now a built-in feature in some products. A new car is better than an old car; a new house is better than a ten-year-old house; used clothes are something to be ashamed about, and so on. Without consumption, businesses would fail. We have moved so far beyond subsistence living, in fact, that we'll spend billions of dollars on novelties like "giggle sticks," special chrome decorations for our cars, and electric toothbrushes.

Apart from the egocentricity and absurdity of rampant consumerism in the face of pressing human needs around the world, there is another issue. It seems to me that we have actually begun to treat people with the same kind of "throwaway" callousness. If a relationship breaks down and doesn't work, we're increasingly ready to throw it away (e.g. — divorce). We can always pick up a new model, it seems, which more suitably fits our current fancy. There seems to be a loss of will and wisdom in how to make close relationships work. We're so accustomed to replacing the old with the new, and with quick solutions, that we don't stick with relationships through repair periods. We give up and discard much too easily. Part of this is due to our society's corresponding emphasis on comfort and personal rights, but part of it is due to seeing people as expendable if they don't meet our needs just the way we want. The cost of throwaway relationships is high, as we'll see. And intense loneliness is only part of it.

Related to this, of course, is the *Playboy* and *Playgirl* philosophy now bought by millions. Sex is separated from intimacy and becomes merely a recreational act. Men and women become merely means for pleasure. Commitment loses it central quality — perseverance. Relationships predicated solely on pleasure and manipulation only foster emptiness and isolation. Throwaway sexual partners may appeal to our fantasies, but the reality is one of continual searching and loneliness.

T.V. Sounds Like T.B.

While the industrial revolution provided the foundation for widespread alienation, the technological revolution has made loneliness a nearly inescapable reality. Technological developments in transportation and mass media have especially affected human relationships.

One of the most significant technological innovations has been the development of television. Television was initially thought of simply as a vehicle for transmitting information and entertainment. For the past six to eight years, however, it has been at the center of intense controversy. Critics charge and give evidence that both the content of television programs and the process of viewing make a difference in how people think and act toward each other. They charge that it promotes violence, unrealistic views of the world, fear, and values that separate people. While the current evidence doesn't totally support these charges, there is a growing body of evidence that television does have some harmful effects on human relationships.

Television certainly seems to be addictive. Ninety-eight percent of American homes contain at least one television set. A recent Nielsen survey found that an average preschooler watches it 23½ hours a week. By the time a typical American reaches eighteen, he has viewed fifteen thousand hours of television. This amounts to 2½ years of his or her life. Adult men watch an average of 24½ hours per week. Adult women are even more dedicated — they're glued to the tube an average of 30 hours and 14 minutes a week. In one home where I stayed for a few days, the television set was turned on first thing in the morning (6:30 A.M.), moved to the dinette area for all meals, and was on *all* day until 11:15 at night! (These were Christian people, by the way).

How does television affect loneliness? First, it promotes aggressive and violent behavior. If something is seen often enough, it becomes normal. Over 70 percent of the stories presented on television contain at least one act of violence. More than 50 percent of all television characters on prime-time engage in violence. The average high school graduate has watched eighteen thousand killings and an equally staggering number of assaultive acts, including increasingly explicit rape scenes. Cartoons have been found to be six times more violent than adult prime-time programs; one violent episode about every two minutes! Conflicts are often ''solved'' by violent resolution — there just isn't enough time to work things out; and it's not as exciting anyway. Psychologists have debated whether such viewing encourages aggression or helps it to be released through identification with the television actors. It appears that young children use aggressive television characters as role models. They become more aggressive after viewing violence. This is especially true for kids who are already more aggressive, from lower-class backgrounds, and from broken homes. The violent activities of teenagers referred to in chapter 2 may be due in part to the models they're being given on television. Increasingly, real-life quarrels between adults seem to be handled violently as well. It is common to hear of spouses or friends ending quarrels with a blast from a gun or the blade of a knife. Violence has never been known to promote intimacy. When television programs display violent behavior as typical, they are only encouraging the breakdown of relationships in real life.

There has been a temporary decline for the past two years in the number of violent incidents on television, due largely to the outcries of the P.T.A. and Action for Children's Television (ACT) groups. The substitute offered by the networks, however, hasn't been much better.

Arguing that they're only giving people what they want, television producers have begun introducing increasingly explicit sex to the home screen. For example, sex is portrayed either casually or in the context of force (i.e. — rape). There is no sense of support for sex within marriage only. Rather, programs like ''Soap'' encourage the idea that sexual encounters should be developed whenever and with whomever one wants. On most television programs, sex outside of the marriage relationship is treated as normal. It's portrayed as a good way to have fun without the hang-ups of commitment. The only problem is that sex without commitment provides short-term physical pleasure and long-term psychological emptiness. It brings anxiety (most often to the woman) and alienation in its wake. Furthermore, recent programming has begun picturing abnormal sexuality, including homosexuality, in a more positive light. This is contrary to God's view of the ideal use of sex between male and female within marriage and can only result in a deep, inner sense of alienation and separation from God.

According to some studies, people who watch large amounts of television have a distorted picture of the real world.[1] This occurs regardless of their educational levels. Heavy viewers see the world as more dangerous than it really is. They're more distrusting of others as a result. They're more fearful and consider it more likely that they'll be involved in some kind of violence. The world of television is oversimplified and gives people the idea that immediate solutions to difficult problems can always be found. This promotes unrealistic expectations of others and a tendency to run away or drop out of relationships when snags are hit and not immediately unsnarled. Patience and problem-solving are not encouraged. Real relationships require trust, perseverance in the face of difficulties, and the willingness to work at understanding if they are to flower into intimacy. Any other way can only result in unresolved conflicts, broken relationships, and loneliness. Indeed, heavy viewers are more apt to have social adjustment problems, to have trouble carrying on conversations, and to be more passive and withdraw from their relationships with people.[2]

At the same time television encourages fear, it also seems to place a premium on cool, sophisticated heroes who have few apparent feelings of genuine tenderness for others. Some have argued that television discourages us from growing up and facing our emotions.[3] Instead it encourages passivity and repression of feelings. Perhaps this accounts for the popularity of Mr. Spock "Star Trek," who is in utter control of himself and his emotions. The fear of becoming an adult leads to an inability to develop long-term emotional commitments, which in turn may lead to fear of marriage, sex without relationship, and interpersonal isolation. Because the absence of deep ties is not satisfying, many people may turn to drugs and heavy television viewing for relief. While these escape routes may provide temporary relief, their only long-lasting by-product is emptiness.

Television also promotes values that seem contrary to positive intimacy building. First of all, advertising fastens itself upon viewers, seeking to manipulate them like objects in order to gain their money. Advertisers spend over $30 billion a year to persuade viewers that their lives will be happier, sexier, and more peaceful if they'll just buy the latest miracle product. Commercials are not known for encouraging integrity. Rather, the half-truths and exaggerations have been found to promote cynicism and distrust toward adult trustworthiness on the part of pre-adolescents. After a while even kids begin to wonder about toothpaste with sex appeal, colognes that promise instant love, whiter than whites, etc. By the time they have turned eighteen and watched 400,000-650,000 commercials, they will either be hooked on the things-make-happiness message or will tend to see life and people through distrusting eyes.

Second, television programs misrepresent family life in any normal sense. Until recently, three-fourths of the leading prime-time characters have been male, single, upper- or middle-class whites in their twenties or thirties. Only one-third intend to be or have been married.[4] Positive family relationships form a vital base for mature and continuing intimacy. Frequently when families are portrayed or talked about, it is in terms of broken relationships.

Third, television downgrades the potentially vital role of religious experience in human lives. Traditional Christianity, especially, is either ignored or displayed in subtley ridiculing terms. For example, when the daughter on "One Day at a Time" became a born-again Christian, she turned into a proud, unkind girl until she saw the light — i.e., what Christianity had done to her. In real life, millions find relief from loneliness through a personal, continuing relationship with God. You wouldn't know it by watching television, despite the recent upsurge in Sunday morning religious programs.

Apart from program content, the addictive nature of television tends to break down relationships in the home. A recent edition of a major encyclopedia showed two pictures alongside its section on the family. The picture captioned as ''family in the early 1900s'' showed family members sitting around a table, conversing with one another. The other picture of a family in the 1970s showed family members isolated in their private worlds, watching televison. They were physically together but interpersonally apart. ''Football widows'' are more than a joke. Many women literally find themselves without a husband from August through January. Their husbands are more in tune with Howard Cosell and Pat Summerall than with those with whom they share a house.

The problem with television is that there is little interaction between viewers. Even when family members watch it together, discussion of the programs is rare. (That may be due to the lack of much to discuss!) Instead of spending time playing together, talking together, and enjoying each other, we sit in splendid isolation, locked into the fantasy world of television. Indeed, one of the signs of having it ''made'' is for a family to have personal television sets for each family member. Then the effort of dialogue and possible disagreement over what show to watch is neatly resolved. Everyone can retreat into his private world and not be bothered by other people. Is it any wonder that husbands and wives can't communicate, and parents and kids feel alienated? Whatever happened to family walks, reading together, playing badminton or horseshoes, family skits and roundtable discussions?

Now, somebody has already objected: ''What about the documentaries and travelogues? What about educational programs? Are you against entertainment?'' No, but I find it rare for families to discipline themselves when it comes to watching television. Besides, reading or playing educational games together will often do as much educational good and provide the added benefits of interaction and togetherness. Or, you could rent a set for special programs. Why not spend an evening telling jokes to each other or playing music together instead of passively listening to canned entertainment?

The usual excuse is "I wish we didn't have a television (but since we have one we're not going to get rid of it)." The best thing, of course, is not to have one at all. Weaning your family off television is really a matter of the will — all of you may suffer some symptoms of withdrawal. Once you kick the habit, though, you'll find there's much more to life than the pale glow of a glass screen. If you can't do it cold turkey, try cutting your family's viewing hours by half and substituting some of the together activities I've suggested. There are many activities and game books available to help you, also. Then as you discover the fun of relating together, you'll probably find the demand for the television lessens until you can quietly slip it out of the house without anyone missing it.

Television is not all bad; there are some benefits. For shut-ins, the elderly widowed, and those who are lonely for other reasons, it can be a welcome companion. It helps time pass and provides the sound of human voices when no one is around. Programs like "Sesame Street" have helped countless children get a head start on basic learning that they probably would have never received otherwise. (Some critics argue that the fast-paced entertainment format of such programs handicaps the child when he goes to school and all there is is a teacher without electronic wizardry.) Also, studies suggest that children will pattern their behavior after prosocial (kind, helping, honest) models as well as antisocial, aggressive ones. Television programs potentially provide a wide variety of information that can be used as a basis for getting to know people. This is especially helpful for those who are shy and have trouble knowing what to talk about. Finally, with the advent of the Christian Broadcasting Network, the 700 Club, P.T.L. Club, and other religious programs, television may provide spiritual encouragement that could otherwise not be obtained.

Values Are Vital

We have already touched upon the important role of values in our discussion of television, but now we'll look at several values that are central in American life: autonomy, achievement, acquisition, and appearance. Each of these values has played an important role in making it possible for most Americans to enjoy the highest standard of living of any people in history.

But they have also promoted division between people, artificiality in relationships, dehumanization, and loneliness. As these values have been gradually secularized, they have become tools of mistrust, insecurity, and fragmentation.

Values are vital because they summarize what we think is important in life. They serve as goals for us. They motivate us. They form the core of our thinking and affect our attitudes toward people. They give us guidance and serve as yardsticks by which we measure ourselves and our relationships. Values serve as the foundation for our choices. They represent our desires. The Bible recognizes the crucial nature of values when it warns us, "Do not love the world or anything in the world" (1 John 2:15), and to "set your hearts on things above" (Colossians 3:1).

There is probably no more compelling idea in modern Western culture than *autonomy*. Autonomy is the desire to be independent and free. This desire runs throughout our whole culture. We're proud of our political freedom, and we increasingly demand freedom in our personal decisions and relationships also. We're taught that dependency is bad. We're encouraged to parent our children so that they will be independent. Autonomy has come to mean being able to do what we want to do when we want to do it, without being restrained by other people's needs or desires. Modern existentialist writers argue that we must be totally free as individuals if we're to break the oppressive, enslaving power of technology. Rejection of obligations and devotion is the existentialist answer. We're even willing to break laws if we feel that they are unfair. We feel it is our *right* to be ourselves and that everyone should be free to ''do his thing'' (as long as it doesn't interfere with our wishes).

As our society has become secularized, turning away from God's ways as decisive values, we have mixed relativism with autonomy. Relativism simply holds that there aren't any absolutes. Rules and regulations are social conveniences without any real authority. No truth is compelling. The individual becomes God. Individual rights are the rule. Whatever works for us is okay.

The results of such unrestrained autonomy aren't difficult to guess. First, God is dispensed with. Or, if we allow Him to remain, He becomes our servant. Autonomous man sees God as either a bothersome limitation or a threat. So we decide He's either dead or senile. In either case *we* become God. In so doing, we may find ourselves very concerned about control. Being able to predict and control things in our world becomes important. Guarding our rights becomes a major way in which we try to keep control.

Second, community and a sense of belonging become more difficult to find because there is a breakdown in authority and trust. We all know that everybody else is out to ''feather his own nest'' also, and that he's trying to build his kingdom using whatever means he feels is right. We can't really trust others because they may simply be using us for their own ends. So, we don't let our real selves be known. We play a deadly game behind pleasant masks — a game of individualism which makes it nearly impossible to form genuine, close relationships with others. Insecure couples, afraid to lose any freedom, choose living arrangements that sacrifice commitment for imagined autonomy. Even within marriages, individual kingdom building may take place. Each partner may be more concerned about preserving his autonomy than he is about giving it up in exchange for mature interdependence and love.

When autonomy becomes our central value we stand alone, unwilling and unable to emotionally connect with others, because we're afraid we might lose our position of unrestrained rule. When a society worships autonomy, people become defensive — they're strangers to one another by choice. Indeed, "loneliness is currently being packaged in an entirely new way — as the price of freedom."[5]

Our society also places a high premium on *achievement*. To achieve or produce is a major sign of our worth. It assures our acceptance. We're taught that getting the highest grades, scoring the most points, making the most sales, writing the most books, earning the most money — getting to the top — is what counts. Winners have lots of connections. Success is our national shrine. Success brings admiration, friends, and loneliness. Person after person who has climbed the shrine to the top has confessed his deep sense of emptiness. Part of the problem is that shrine-climbers often view others as objects, useful as toeholds to the top. Others view them as status-enhancers. Relationships often become mutual manipulation — mutually helpful to be sure — but without the genuineness and caring out of which intimacy is constructed.

In addition, success normally requires careful conformity to role expectations. Those who enter the achievement race usually find themselves caught in very role-specific relationships. This means that they seldom have knowledge or are known outside their positions and functions. They are related to as celebrities, presidents, teachers, janitors, or key punch operators first, and as people second or not at all. The vice-principal of the high school I attended was mightily feared. Well-embellished rumor had it that he could lick any kid in school, and it was wise not to be sent to his office. He was the bouncer, the disciplinarian. It wasn't until years later when I revisited the school that I suddenly realized he was really a nice person who had been placed in a role he probably didn't relish but had to play. He talked warmly and kindly to me that day, and I saw beyond his role.

We do the same thing to teachers. Even college students tend to see teachers as "textbooks wired for sound" — not as real people with real hobbies, families, and needs. Some students are very reluctant to be exposed to the real person behind the role. Most seem to feel special appreciation when teachers step out of their roles and allow themselves to be seen — when they play a round of volleyball or invite students (as *people*) into their homes.

Often we do a disservice to those who have achieved positions of leadership and prominence by not letting them be human. We like to elevate achievers into heroes. Heroes have to be more than human. Anything less is disillusioning. Consequently, we surround our heroes with auras of perfection and expect them to have no weaknesses. In requiring them to be more than human, we make them less than human. When even their close friends start treating them as heroes, they are only insuring isolation and loneliness. Those who have achieved need friends who accept them just for being Jimmy, Sally, or George. They need those to whom they can talk freely without being quoted or misquoted. They even need those who can disagree with them and be honest in their feelings without being seen as threats, because they are friends.

Even among those who have it made — they've climbed to the top — there is artificiality in most relationships. A great amount of time and thought is given to being in the "right" clubs, being seen with the "right" people, doing the "right" things. Conversation is carefully measured and limited to generally superficial and brief interaction.

An achievement-centered society tends to breed competitiveness. There has to be a standard of some kind, a measure, in order to know if we've achieved. Normally that standard is other people. Instead of helping each other, we easily get locked into games of one-upmanship in order to guard our fragile sense of self-worth. The result is distancing between people. Competitors can't be trusted. We often exist in uneasy ambivalence toward others, needing them but also feeling threatened.

One of the major symbols of achievement in our society is

acquisition. As a guiding value, acquisition focuses us on things as the way to happiness. Having the newest, biggest, best, or most becomes a kind of psychological security blanket for many. Clothes, houses, cars, property, and cash are the way to acceptance. If we have them, we are worth getting to know. The problem is that this also means people are related to in terms of what they own rather than who they are. We become very careful to display those goods which tell others they would benefit from relating to us. Acquisition gives us a measure of control, also. Those who don't have what we have either don't seek our friendship or can be summarily dismissed. People are treated as commodities, nuisances, and threats. We can look down upon, reject, and dehumanize those who have less as "no good," "lazy," or "worth-less." Although this approach may partially restore our sense of self-esteem, it also launches us into an ocean with no shoreline. Manufacturers will always make sure there are new items to be bought — new inventions, new revisions. They make us feel inadequate, unattractive, and less than complete without their soap, mouthwash, toothpaste, and hairspray.

It's easy to start focusing on protection of our acquisitions. The more we have, the more others want what we have also; this can lead to a sense of defensiveness about people, feeling that all people want is to get out of us what they can. Perhaps the most dramatic, but not the only, illustration of the effects of acquisition on loneliness is billionaire Howard Hughes. Hughes spent most of the truly wealthy years of his life as a recluse, isolated from true friendship. He had everything that our society says is necessary for happiness. He died financially rich but emotionally poor and lonely.

A side effect of centering on acquisition has been the quantification of value. What is really important can be measured. The more there is of something, the more valuable it is. Numbers count, individuals don't. Bigger is better. Within Christian circles this is seen in the focus on ten-thousand-member churches and churches with multimillion dollar facilities and budgets. The impression is given that these churches are the places where God is really at work. These are the places to belong to. Large churches often provide a gathering place for groups of people with special needs, where they can meet others that understand them and their life situations. Often, however, it is in the smaller gatherings that God's Spirit is making the deepest *qualitative* changes. When God called the people of Israel to be His own, He declared that it was not because they were mighty in number or in resources, but because He loved them and would show His power through them. It is usually in smaller gatherings that the individual is most thoroughly cared for and included. He is not just another number in the crowd. A "bigger is better" emphasis can also promote isolation. Though many large churches have various small-group gatherings, it is easier in them to relate to others as part of an impersonal organization, and to remain relatively anonymous, than it is in a smaller church.

A fourth central value in American society is *appearance*. Americans spend billions of dollars each year on cosmetics so that they will look more desirable. Gray hair and wrinkles are feared, not just because they remind us that life doesn't last forever, but because people might think we're past our prime. We may also fear that our husband or wife won't love us anymore once we've lost our youthful appearance.

At the earliest ages we treat those who look better, better. Teachers often evaluate physically attractive kids more highly, regardless of their actual intelligence levels. Kids who appear homely or dress poorly are downgraded. They're typically seen as less capable and as having more behavior problems, even when this is not objectively supported. Kids like to play with "the beautiful people" more than with those who aren't as attractive. Attractive children and adults are more often chosen to be leaders by their respective peer groups. This creates some problems. For the unattractive it means repeated experiences of feeling left out and unwanted. For the attractive it means greater expectations; people expect them to have super personalities, to be warm and sociable, to be better companions and spouses, to perform better sexually, and so forth. When they don't meet expectations, they're judged severely. For example, rather than being seen as shy, they're viewed as stuck up; or, rather than being tired and needing to be alone, they're seen as cold and aloof. These great expectations can lead to great rejection.

Close relationships are built on what's *in* the package, not on how it's wrapped. Kindness, caring, ability to affirm, dialogue, and disclosure are the essential ingredients of intimacy. Focus on appearances encourages us to commit the "halo" fallacy — to think that because things look good they are good. We ought to know better, but we're encouraged to think otherwise. Business can't sell the internals as readily as the wrappings, so it spends billions convincing us that if the wrappings are right we'll be loved and accepted.

A fifth major value which affects most Americans today is *actualization*. As we indicated in chapter 1, thousands of people are spending millions of dollars in the quest for self-fulfillment. People are incessantly searching for peace and happiness. Due to the pervasive influence of secular psychology, which has replaced God for many, and Eastern mystical religions, people have turned inward. Psychologists have replaced pastors for many people who don't really have serious emotional problems but are unhappy with who they are and are expecting more out of themselves and life. One is struck by the observation that many who would have been considered "put together" fifty years ago are involved in deep, inner exploration which all too often seems to bring anxiety and confusion instead of actualization. In many cases, the quest for self-actualization results in the abandonment of spouses and families, who restrict the free-flying quest of the searchers with down-to-earth responsibilities. Instead of fulfillment, the search for self and happiness has brought separation, sadness, and loneliness for many. One can't help wonder if the intensity of the search in modern culture is simply an attempt to fill the inner emptiness that has come with the removal of God from many lives. Is the search for self really a search for God?

Even within the Christian community we are more likely to hear sermons on self-fulfillment than on being God's servants, on happiness rather than on hell, on salvation as relief from distresses rather than as redemption from sin. Historically, a Christian's self-fulfillment has been seen as a by-product of commitment to the purpose of following God's leading wholeheartedly. That seems to be changing in today's church.

Cities and Companionship

To get a clear picture of the magnitude of the urban revolution, we need to realize that from 1900-1970 the world's population doubled, but *urban* population increased *six* times. There were 224 million living in cities in 1900, compared to 1.3 *billion* in 1970. And the trend is accelerating. In 1900 there were 11 cities with a million residents; by 1985 there will be 273! In 1950, there were 2 cities with 10 million people; by 1985 there will be at least 17. The entire world is going through a revolution that will profoundly affect human relationships.

Although cities put millions of people physically close together, there are several factors about large urban configurations that seem to foster isolation and loneliness. Our task is to find ways to overcome those things about urbanization that have promoted broken connections between people.

The most obvious thing about cities is that they are crowded and confining. Crowding seems to affect how people behave, though the picture is a bit complicated. Early study of crowded animals found that they broke down physically, socially, and emotionally.[6] Some animals died unexpectedly. Aggression and antisocial behavior, including "gang" rapes, occurred at alarming rates. Among humans, crowding seems to increase feelings of anxiety, stress, and hostility toward others *when* it is experienced as a loss of personal control. People who have grown up in a densely settled area don't show the same effects. Cities are also places of concentrated activity and noise.

People who live on streets with heavy traffic are less likely to

use the fronts of their homes to socialize. Their sense of personal
territory rarely extends beyond their apartment or house. In
comparison, people living on lightly used streets socialize a
great deal more in front of their homes, and they see the whole
block as their territory.[7] Loud noise that hearers can't predict or
control (for example, traffic noise, horns tooting, sirens screaming, and airplanes roaring overhead) leads to a lower tolerance
for frustration and a lower quality performance on complex
tasks.[8] In order to cope with the mere presence of people, noise,
and other happenings that abound in everyday city life, people
try to filter out stimuli. They place a greater emphasis on privacy
and anonymity. While they may not be able to control the
number of people living or working around them, and the other
sights and sounds which intrude into their lives, they can regulate their interactions to some extent. For example, privacy is
helped by the agreement that people make appointments for
social gatherings. The small-town habit of just "dropping by"
is usually seen as an unwanted intrusion in the city — it's
another unpredictable violation of privacy. People in cities also
shut off interaction by avoiding eye glances. In effect they are
saying, "I may have to walk by you, but as far as I'm (emotionally) concerned, you don't exist." Another example of how
people compensate for stimulus overload is the tendency to
ignore events which have low personal priority. Often this trans-
lates into an unwillingness to stop and help someone who may
be in trouble or need because he is a stranger, and we "don't
want to get involved." These and other coping strategies which
promote privacy help us to compensate for the unavoidable
intrusions into our personal space that mark life in urban settings.

When privacy is highly emphasized, intimate relations are
difficult to develop. People often feel so emotionally drained
from simply being around people that they want to be alone in
the privacy of their homes or apartments after a day at work.
They don't feel much like making the effort it takes to develop

close relationships. They are caught in the emotional bind of wanting to be apart from others but also needing them to fill the emptiness in their lives.

Fear of *crime* in the city also causes a great deal of mistrust. Where poverty abounds, crime is usually common as well. For people living in poorer centers of metropolitan areas, life is one of anxiety about the motives of other people. Though crime is by no means confined to urban centers, it does tend to be higher there than in suburban parts of the metropolis (which in turn is higher than in small towns and rural areas). Although crime rates have decreased a bit in the past two to three years, the image is still there. When you don't really know who your neighbor is, can't depend on the physical security of your home, and know of others who have been robbed or raped, an underlying level of anxiety, suspicion, and tentativeness enters into social relationships. This makes the development of acquaintances who can become close friends very difficult for those who may be especially in need — singles, newly divorced, widowed, and the elderly. One even thinks twice about inviting neighbors into his home to get better acquainted.

Finally, the *physical design* of residential and business areas may also encourage isolation. Apartments that are built to insure the greatest amount of privacy and security usually decrease opportunities for people to meet each other. High-rise buildings are infamous for their lack of meeting space, and for the long, barracklike corridors which discourage interaction. In lower income areas these high-rise designs, which psychologically separate residents, seem to encourage crime. In low-rise, two-and three-story buildings, crime is lessened, and positive social contact is heightened when the design includes courtyards and play areas for children.

Urbanization, individualism, and the industrial/commercial value of efficiency have resulted in residential and office designs that are financially profitable but socially bankrupt. Apartment hallways, supermarket aisles, and factorylike offices have replaced front porches, the corner store with chairs around the stove, and shops arranged to encourage conversation. Modern architecture has done much to prevent or inhibit interaction in space-conscious urban settings. The development of suburban sprawl with its emphasis on automobiles and private space has also promoted interpersonal isolation. Neighborliness is discouraged by the physical separation of individual lots. The emphasis on fast movement by means of automobiles and freeways discourages more casual interaction that walking or horseback riding once encouraged.[9]

There is evidence, however, that adjustments are beginning to take place and that new forms of community are emerging in urban America. These opportunities to belong and develop relationships seem to be more prevalent among people with similar professions and special interests than between neighbors who live close together. In urban settings we are beginning to see everyone from modern railroad enthusiasts to photography buffs, from groups of nurses to business executives, grouping together, enjoying each other through their common interests. Also, many new apartment and condominium developments are planning social activities into the life of the complexes and designing physical spaces to encourage positive social relations. As these new forms of association mature and expand, it is possible that our view of the city will also change. Though privacy requirements will probably always be high, it seems there will be more and easier opportunities for social intimacy than in the past.

5

THEY DON'T WANT
ME ON THEIR TEAM

Though much about American society promotes loneliness, it's neither an automatic nor a perpetual experience. Our society's values and social conditions encourage social isolation, but they don't guarantee that everyone will experience loneliness. The extent to which we absorb our society's perspectives makes a big difference. Also, other events have much to do with our direct experiences of loneliness.

Perhaps one of the deepest needs that we have as human beings is the need to belong. Because we are fundamentally social beings, not belonging is a crushing experience. When those whom we want to be friends with, to belong to, fail to accept and value us, we feel cut off, disconnected, and lonely. As we have already noted, the need to belong can lead to extreme behaviors, including drug-taking and delinquency. Lonely college freshmen have endured all kinds of humiliation, including beatings and death, in their attempts to belong to fraternities or sororities.

The feeling of not belonging regularly occurs when we move to a new place. We discover that people have different values or don't need us. We feel like islands with no bridges. People who are socially confident and emotionally stable prior to moves may go through a period of self-doubt and turmoil until they begin to find others to connect with, who return their overtures. It is, therefore, normal for people to feel lonely for the first twelve to eighteen months after a move, until they have become part of a new, supportive social network.

Not belonging is also the result of rejection by those we wish to relate to. Not belonging due to rejection is worse than simply not having anyone physically available to relate to. It strikes at the very heart of who we are. Rejection communicates to us that we are not worth knowing. Rejection means loneliness because it leaves us feeling worthless as well as friendless.

Rejection may be communicated in several ways. We may try to initiate a relationship with a person or group and find that our initiatives are not returned. Perhaps we begin to sense that we're always the one who is making the contacts and extending the invitations. Or we may begin to feel as though we're being avoided. Groups often have entrance requirements and may tell us outright that we're not good enough to belong. Within parent-child relationships, rejection may be communicated nonverbally or through statements like, "I wish you'd never been born."

The significance of rejection extends beyond the pain of immediate loneliness, because it affects the way we feel about ourselves. It introduces doubt into our self-concept in such a direct way that we cannot ignore it. Each of us has a mental picture made up of descriptive labels — we're tall or short, sociable or shy, witty or wool-headed, optimists or pessimists. We also evaluate ourselves with regard to our self-concept. How we feel about ourselves is what psychologists call self-esteem. Our self-esteem depends largely upon the way in which people who are emotionally important to us feel about us. The more highly we value someone, the more effect his comments and evaluations have upon us. If we are rejected by those we value, we're likely to plunge into a pit of searching and self-doubt. This blocks our ability to form new relationships. People who feel bad about themselves are more likely to have emotional and social difficulties. They're more easily hurt by others. They find it harder to receive or to give love. They feel more isolated and less able to change things. Rejection virtually destroys our capacity for intimacy because it tells us we are worthless. It asserts that worthless people aren't wanted and would only be rejected in the future if they tried to reach out as they have in the past. Rejection easily freezes people into loneliness.

It is also important to realize that we may at times incorrectly interpret the lack of initiative on the part of others toward us as active rejection. Often this is not the case. Rather, people may already have their fill of close relationships and just not feel able to develop and maintain another one. Or they may feel that due to our position or reputation we have all the friends we need. Or they may lack the social confidence to reach out to us. This, of course, does not ease the pain of not belonging, but it does give us more hope than actual rejection. One young lady described this feeling:

> I realized I had been expecting people to come to me, to approach me.... I really wanted someone to approach me because I had taken the initiative all my life.... I wanted someone, just once, to make the first move toward me.[1]

Once she realized that her slip into passivity was causing loneliness, she began reaching out again to others and found her loneliness was resolved.

This chapter will examine the powerful effect that relations with parents, peers, and spouses have upon loneliness. To the extent that we feel accepted in these relationships we will not feel intensely or chronically lonely. Because of their influence upon us during the formative years of our psyche, parents and childhood peers have a significant impact upon long-term loneliness.

Parents and Kids

Normally, parents form a very strong bond with their newborn children. A mother's attachment to her child may well be the strongest connection made between humans. The quality of the early parent-child bond is crucial for all subsequent attachments the child will make. If the bond is strong, the child will develop in an atmosphere of acceptance and security. He will be able to develop relationships based on trust because he has experienced trust in the home.

How is a good parent-child bond formed? Extensive studies of bonding between parents and children have revealed that it is important for mothers to touch and explore their babies and to constantly care for them in the hours immediately after birth.[2] It also appears that infants are programmed to respond to the human face. They respond to a moving face and sounds near their ears. Newborns see best at about nine to twelve inches. This is exactly the distance between mother's and infant's eyes when the mother breastfeeds or holds the baby! Mothers report that once their baby looks at them they feel much closer to him.

Mothers who have extended contact during the first hours and days after birth hold their babies so there is more eye to eye contact, fondle them more, and are more reluctant to leave their babies with someone else. The babies cry less and smile and laugh more. At five years of age they score higher on language tests and have higher IQ's than babies born under standard hospital rules of minimum mother-child contact.

New evidence also suggests that viewing the birth process increases the sense of bonding. Involvement of the father (as encouraged by the LaMaze and Bradley natural childbirth methods) seems to increase his sense of attachment to the child and facilitates family adjustments made necessary by the child's arrival.

Birth technique, of course, is not a magical guarantee of subsequent parent-child relations. *More crucial than any technique is the attitude of the parents toward the child.* Unfortunately, all children are not wanted. And there lies the beginning of heartache and loneliness for countless people. Parental rejection forms a foundation of shifting sand, of doubt and insecurity, in a child's life.

Shyrone's mother didn't want him to be born. During her pregnancy, she was heavily into drugs. She hoped that her baby would die if she didn't eat properly and took enough drugs. Shyrone lived. His mother then refused to play with, talk to, or pay any attention to him. By 9 months, Shyrone kept curling into the fetal position. He was smaller than most 3 month old babies. At about 3 years he began to walk, but ate like an animal and was clearly abnormal. At age 4 he still couldn't talk.[3]

Parents reject their children for various reasons. For some, the child was unplanned and is an obstruction to the fulfillment of their dreams. They may have been saving money to buy a new house or to go on a major trip. Or the child may be viewed simply as a curtailment to their freedom. They may resent the responsibilities of caretaking, the special arrangements and interrupted nights. For others, the child was not what they expected. I have seen some parents so dead sure that their child was going to be a boy or a girl that I've shuddered to learn it didn't turn out the way they *knew* it would. Some parents handle their disappointment by giving neutral or adapted names (Louise for Louis, or Harry for Harriet) or by treating the child like a member of the expected gender. Girls may be treated like tomboys, and boys may be encouraged in traditionally feminine behaviors or allowed to wear their hair very long.

Then there are the dashed expectations that congenitally deformed children bring. There is inevitably a struggle that parents go through of shock, denial, despair, and rejection. For some the struggle takes a long time, and acceptance is painfully slow. For others, resolution may never come.

Parental rejection of the child is expressed in various ways. The most dramatic forms are physical abuse or neglect:

Five year old Wayne was accidentally discovered by firemen when they responded to a call to the house where he had been kept prisoner. His mother and her boyfriend had locked him in an upstairs room to teach him a lesson. The problem was that he had been locked in for three years. He had been given food handed in by the mother. Bruise marks indicated that he had been beaten, apparently for crying. Wayne was verbally incoherent and frightened of anyone. He showed severe mental, social, and emotional disturbances.

While not all parental abuse is this dramatic, the battered child syndrome has become an all-too-familiar sight. Almost 2 million American children are victims of child abuse each year. Child abuse is the most common cause of death from birth to age five. Abuse has dramatically increased during the past 10 years. It happens most in the Midwest and least in the South. In California alone there are over forty thousand cases reported each year. The most common signs of abuse or neglect are physical signs such as fracture, unusual burns, or injuries around the mouth, and lethargy, or "failure to thrive," during the first year of life. About 50 percent of those children who fail to "thrive" have had inadequate calorie intake or love.[4] Less obvious forms of child abuse, not included in the formal term "battered child syndrome," include sexual abuse and absence of love or nurturing affection.

It's important to note here that though child abuse may be interpreted as rejection, it is not always intended as such. More often it is an impulsive reaction to multiple stresses, including prolonged crying by the child, by parents who in their own infancies had very little nurturing love and who see the child's behavior in unrealistic (often moralistic — willful, spoiled) ways. For an estimated 80 percent of those parents, counseling that helps them understand their impulses and the child's needs, combined with a variety of support options such as crisis nurseries and therapeutic day care centers, eliminate the abuse. Although data are not available at this point, it is interesting to note that the rise in abuse has paralleled the rise of one-parent families in which multiple demands and minimal supportive outlets face a single parent.

In addition to child abuse, parental rejection may be expressed in other ways that turn a child inward and make his world insecure. A number of psychiatrists have recently pointed to the emergence of narcissism as a major problem. Narcissism is egocentric self-love, expressed by a grandiose sense of self-importance and preoccupation with fantasies of unlimited power. A Greek legend provides us with the classic portrayal of narcissism. Narcissus was a beautiful youth who pined away with love for his own image as reflected in a pool. Narcissism blocks the ability of people to love others. Narcissists feel empty and alone. In actuality, the narcissist has low self-esteem and is totally dependent upon the constant admiration and praise of others. He is easily depressed by slight rejection and falls apart over little illnesses, because it seems to him that his world is falling apart when these things happen. Though they may seem very socially attractive at first, narcissists lack emotional depth, seem unable to feel genuine sadness, and generally have parisitic or manipulative relationships with others.[5] Often they are sexually promiscuous. They have an underlying sense of abandonment, worthlessness, and loneliness. Our society generally encourages narcissism by emphasizing superficial ways to gain acceptance and approval, such as by accumulating material goods. More specifically, however, narcissists usually have parents who are cold and rejecting. Usually their mothers appear to function well but are emotionally callous, indifferent, and highly aggressive toward them.[6] The result is a continuous search for approval and an inability to form deep relationships because of an abiding sense of hostility toward people, hostility that doesn't appear on the surface but becomes obvious over time in a relationship.

Parents can communicate rejection both nonverbally and verbally. With young infants it may take the form of little or no cuddling and physical contact, such as happened to Shyrone. Infants seem to be built with the need to be touched and held. They also prefer the human face to other kinds of stimulation. Mere provision of food and physical needs is not enough. Infants in an institution that provided more-than-adequate physical care but gave no opportunity for adequate cuddling were found to be unable to speak, walk, or feed themselves. A tragic 37 percent of them died within their first two years due to lack of human contact and love.[7] Infants need to be held and played with if they are to be able to form intimate attachments.

Some parents feel that you should never pick an infant up when he cries because it will ''spoil'' him. To the contrary, picking infants up when they show signs of distress, and appropriately meeting their needs, results in less crying, whining, and demanding. Children whose needs are ignored due to such a moralistic approach develop an underlying sense of distrust and anger toward the world. Some will say about their infant's crying, ''All he wants its to be picked up,'' and regard that as an insufficient need. In truth, it appears that an important cause of crying in the first three months of life is the need to be cuddled.[8] This source of crying is observed when the baby is fed, dry, and not suffering from any other discomfort, but still crys. Crying promptly stops when the baby is held and cuddled. Refusal to see holding as a legitimate need leaves the child with a sense of abandonment.

Spending time playing with and listening to children, being available, is also an important sign of acceptance. One recent study showed that fathers average only seven and one-half minutes a week alone with their junior high sons. Taking time symbolizes to the child that he is important and worthwhile. It communicates that he is wanted and loved. It also provides occasions for the child to learn *how* to relate to someone he loves. One of the traps that materialism has set is the notion that we can make up for lack of parental presence, while one or both parents work to get ahead, by giving our children things. Kids need their parents more than toys and things. Increasingly, both parents work and children are left either on their own or with a variety of babysitters. This is true in our neighborhood. The kids are bored and starved for adult attention and affection. They eat up the time that my wife or I spend talking, teasing, and horsing around with them. It's not uncommon for me to be met by a group of 10-14 year olds wanting to wrestle or play when I come home from work. Nor is it unusual for them to come to us with a problem and ask for advice. The tragedy is that their own parents are rarely available because they are either physically or emotionally absent.

Parents sometimes openly express their rejection as well. I know of some people whose parents have said such things to them as, "I really didn't want to have you," or "You were an accident — we didn't want any more kids." Those kinds of comments cripple for life. They make a child feel unwanted and alone. It's like dropping the bottom out of an airplane and expecting the passengers to fly. It removes the foundation of security and support that is so essential for healthy emotional development. It triggers a lifetime of trying to prove that one is good enough to be loved. Tragically, such rejection makes it difficult or even impossible for one to receive and accept love. An underlying fear of further rejection causes such a person to dwell on hurts and signs that he really isn't loved. The result, of course, is a lifetime of isolation and loneliness.

Other significant statements of rejection may include such comments as, "I can't wait until you're old enough to get out on your own," or "He'll never amount to anything." I'm appalled at the number of times I have heard parents make such disparaging comments about their children to other people, often while the children are present. They act as though their child can't hear or doesn't exist. The kids get the message.

Sometimes parents convey rejection by the way they discipline. Extremely harsh discipline tells a child that his parents not only don't like what he's done, but also that they don't like him! Extreme permissiveness may tell a child that his parents really don't care about what he does or what happens to him. Kids from very permissive homes often have doubts about whether their parents really love them; frequently they express a desire for more-definite and enforced guidelines. Interestingly, children with high self-esteem are more likely to come from homes which have explicit and consistently enforced rules.

Perhaps one of the worst kinds of disciplinary techniques is the withdrawal of love. At the least it promotes an uncertainty and a search for approval that lasts into adulthood. Adults who are afraid to risk disapproval have a difficult time allowing themselves to be authentic in close relationships. Intimacy is blocked. At its worst, love withdrawal leads to the crippling anxiety and feelings of isolation of the chronically lonely. This is especially true if the withdrawal involves threats of abandonment. One woman revealed that:

> I used to threaten him (4 year old son) with the Hartley Road Boys' Home, which isn't a Home anymore; and since then, I haven't been able to do it; but I can always say I shall go down town and see about it, you know. And Ian says, "Well, if I'm going with Stuart (7) it won't matter"; so I say, "Well, you'll go to different ones — you'll go to one Home and *he'll* go to another." But it really got him worried, you know, and I really got him ready one day and I thought I'll take him for a walk round, as if I was going, you know, and he really was worried. In fact, I had to bring him home, he started to cry. He saw I was in earnest about it — he *thought* I was, anyway. And now I've only got to threaten him. I say "It won't take me long to get you ready."[9]

Parents may also threaten to leave home or commit suicide. There are even reports of attempted suicides after threats were made to the children. This is obviously a deep shock to the child, removes the core of security upon which intimacy is built, and leads to chronic anxiety about losing love and loved ones. It's difficult to estimate what percentage of parents use threats of abandonment as a disciplinary procedure. However, we can safely guess that the use of love withdrawal in general has increased with the general decrease in physical discipline in our society.

One other way in which parents may affect the long-term

loneliness of their children is by being overprotective. Some argue that overprotectiveness is really a camouflaged form of rejection that helps a parent cover up his deepest feelings about his child. We won't argue that point one way or the other. The issue for us is the isolation and anxiety it introduces into a child's life. I know of one mother who was so overprotective of her year-old son that she wouldn't let him crawl on the floor — he always was to be in his playpen, his toys had to be washed every day, and he could have no contact with another child if there was the slightest hint of a cold. Another mother insisted that the sand in her son's sandbox be sterilized. The normal pattern is to carefully circumscribe the world of an overprotected child so that everything is predictable and no harm can be done. This carries over into the child's social life. Parents may prevent him from playing with other kids (or at most one or two *very* carefully selected playmates). The problem is that the child grows up not knowing how to live with the ups and downs of normal life and usually adopts a fear orientation. It's also likely that he will have difficulty relating to other people because he's never had an opportunity to develop and practice normal social skills in his highly limited social world.

Parents also need to be careful not to compare one child with another. Inevitably somebody comes up on the short end, feeling inferior and unloved. Those who insist on talking about one child's great exploits, while neglecting or criticizing another child, are simply driving the loser into self-doubt and insecurity. Parents with adopted children need to be especially careful to affirm adoption as a special decision that shows how very much they wanted and love their child. Covering up about adoptions almost inevitably leads to tremendous emotional shock, identity crisis, and feelings of being adrift with no one to really belong to on the part of the adopted child. Being straightforward at an early age is the best policy. Being careful not to overemphasize who got what from whom (blue eyes from grandma) with regard to natural-born children in the family is also important.

Sticks and Stones

When I was a kid, we were taught that the best comeback for any ridicule or teasing directed at us by other kids was to reply in sing-song fashion, "Sticks and stones may break my bones, but names will never hurt me." Somehow that never seemed to be my experience. The words and actions of other kids really *did* hurt at times. Acceptance and rejection by our peers have a large impact on our feelings of loneliness. Several studies have shown that children who are rejected by their playmates have higher rates of crime and mental illness later in life. Being made to feel unwanted by others hurts deeply, whether we're kids, teens, or adults. Jane remarked to me that her most lonely experience was "being with a fairly large group of people, who all seemed to go together and were having fun, but they ignored me." Ted likewise said that he had been loneliest one time when he thought he had no friends at all. Even though he realized it wasn't true, he still felt it.

One of the reasons people are rejected is that they aren't skilled in the things that count with their peers. I'm sure many of us have experienced the breathtaking trauma of choosing teams for some game, and being chosen last. After a few times of being picked last, and then only because the teacher said a team *had* to take him, a kid gets the idea that he's not wanted! That's why it's wise for parents to help their children develop at least passable skills in areas valued by other kids. Usually that involves some level of physical prowess. Fortunately or unfortunately, athletics is a key to general acceptance, even among kids. Whether it's climbing trees, running races, kicking balls, batting, playing tag, arm wrestling, or whatever, teach your child to develop whatever abilities he has to some moderate level of acceptability. Kids who can hardly stand up without falling down usually have a tough time with their peers. As time goes on, the most desired skills change, but until adulthood physical appearance or performance are powerful values in our society. Certainly a parent shouldn't overemphasize this area. Development of musical appreciation and skills, mental abilities, and a variety of hobbies is often a significant bridge into other people's lives. They shouldn't be neglected. I heard recently of a man who had developed one new skill or hobby each year for the past twenty-five years. Needless to say, he was neither bored nor boring. He had an easy time finding things to discuss with others.

Another reason for peer rejection is "looking or acting different." Kids can be ruthless at times. They'll very loudly call attention to big ears, buck teeth, freckles, skin color, obesity, and more-severe physical defects. That's one of the reasons millions of teens go through "Clearasil Calisthenics" each morning to make sure they'll pass the peer pimple test.

Greg had a very lonely childhood. The kids in his class at school and at his church were always taunting him about his big ears. They really weren't so big, they just stuck out. His crew cut, which was in style, didn't help matters. It got so he would avoid a lot of his classmates so he didn't have to hear teasing about "elephant ears." He had very few friends until he later demonstrated abilities they valued.

The situation is worse for those with serious congenital defects. If the disability is bad enough, we simply place the "reject" in an institution where we don't have to deal with our feelings. We can simply reject them by forgetting them. And yet, removal of individuals from their family and community networks can easily foster loneliness, depending on their emotional capacities.

For those with less severe handicaps, socially derogatory attitudes which communicate "You're weird," "You're not as good as the rest of us," or "I'm glad I'm not you" lead to self-rejection and social withdrawal. Several of my students did an interesting little study to see how people would respond to an apparently handicapped person in a wheelchair. One of the things they found was that people treated the student who acted disabled as if she couldn't think or wasn't there. One waitress took orders for them by asking one of the "normals" what *she* (the girl in the wheelchair) wanted to eat.

A third major reason we may be rejected by our peers is

because we may think differently and have varying values. Rhonda's experience isn't atypical: "I really was lonely when I was in the 10th and 11th grades. My best friend didn't want to be my best friend anymore because I didn't smoke or drink, and I didn't have a boyfriend. I didn't have *any other* friends, besides her." Carey has felt isolated and lonely because she is "over-conscientious and I've cut myself off from the people at work because they say I work too hard."

Christian teens have a special problem with loneliness due to different values. They may have to endure being called "Holy Joe" or "Pious Priscilla." Their peers often make fun of them for being naive and missing all the "good things" in life. They may be avoided if they take a stand against alcohol, cocaine, marijuana, cheating, premarital sex, and punk rock. Solid Christians, willing to identify themselves as such, are hard to find. So the teen may feel totally isolated. Without strong support groups at school and church, and without enjoyable activities, many Christian kids buckle under the pressure. The intense need to belong and to be valued forces many into agonizing compromise and subsequent rejection of the values that have caused them such pain.

Adults are not immune either. Usually Christian adults give other reasons, such as job security, for compromising. That may be part of it, but it's only part. Underlying compromise is the fear of being rejected if we're too different. This is becoming a significant day-to-day issue in our post-Christian society. Are we willing to experience the loneliness of not belonging because we have values that are different and act on them? If there is any form of alienation that we might argue *ought* to be part of the Christian's experience, it would be cultural alienation — being cut off from the core values of our secular society. If we fear the loneliness of rejection by those who reject Christ, and conform out of fear, we will risk the ultimate disapproval of our Savior. Christians don't need to disagree with everyone and everything just for principle's sake, of course. Rather, we need to carefully examine the central values of our society, discern where they conflict with consistent Christianity, and risk loneliness.

Another significant cause of loneliness is conflict between friends. One teenager said the loneliest experience she had ever had was "when I had a fight with my three best friends in high school and they spent the night over at one of their houses without me." Loneliness is often ushered in due to seemingly insurmountable breakdowns in close friendships. We may find ourselves deeply at odds with someone we have spent hours of time with — time laughing, talking, playing, crying, praying, and planning. And then it's gone. Perhaps it was a small misunderstanding that grew into major proportions because it was told to others, or an unkind word that struck at the heart of us, or a disagreement in principle over some issue. Whatever it was, forgiveness was either not asked or it was not granted. And the pride set in — we probably called it "rights." The lines hardened. We avoided each other, didn't talk. And a friendship was lost. So was a sense of belonging, of being able to share without fear of rejection.

"Mrs. Adams Says I Ain't No Good at Spellun."

Poor Kevin can't seem to keep up with his class in either spelling or math. His handwriting, however, is getting to be quite excellent. It ought to be with all the practice he's getting — writing each misspelled word ten times! Unfortunately, his teacher has not been too quiet about her evaluation of his abilities, and the other kids in the class have picked up that Kevin is "dumb" and probably won't go on to the next grade.

Teachers and other authority figures have a significant influence upon kids throughout their school years. Several fascinating studies have shown that teachers tend to get what they expect. If they think that certain kids will do very well, the kids do better than those the teachers don't think so highly of. If teachers expect misbehavior they get it. This is not to say that teacher expectations are completely arbitrary — there is a high level of discernment among experienced teachers. The point is still that some students are treated within a context of false expectations.

In American society, where achievement is a top value and academic performance is an indication of achievement potential, evaluations by the teacher that a student *can't* make it can be devastating. It is especially damaging when this message is conveyed to other kids or other teachers up the line. Certainly we need to be realistic and not encourage those who lack specific abilities to think they'll become what they realistically won't. At the same time, teachers and the school systems of our country need to develop ways to cope with the "nonachievers" so that they don't feel worthless, become isolated, and drop out. That sort of progressive rejection experience felt grade after grade can only make a person feel marginal and intensely alienated.

Although it is less frequent, teachers sometimes cultivate rejection by overemphasizing the academic skills of their high achievers. Matthew's teachers constantly praised him as their "star" throughout grade school and junior high. He began to seek their approval and became more and more distant from his peers. He is currently in college but is almost totally isolated from his family — he spends hours alone in his room and doesn't relate to his brother, sisters, or parents. He has no friends; they stopped calling long ago after their invitations were repeatedly turned down. Matthew is brilliant, but his life is empty.

This is not the place for a detailed exploration of how to encourage self-worth while simultaneously developing and evaluating competency. Volumes have been written about it in the fields of educational philosophy and psychology. We need to remember, though, that the thousands of hours a child spends in schools affect his ability to form intimate relationships. The skills he learns or doesn't learn affect his self-confidence and his social worth. They determine who he will meet and the potential for relationships he will have. His social interactions in school, whether of belonging or exclusion, help set a life pattern of intimacy or isolation.

Marriage: Garden or Gravel Pit?

If marriage holds the greatest potential for deep and satisfying intimacy on all levels, it also has the greatest potential for intense hurts and loneliness. Spouses normally reveal more of themselves to each other than they do to anyone else. By living together day after day, each begins to see the torn pieces in the other's formal mask. Dreams are shared; so are discouragements. Anxieties and fears that we've never revealed may be expressed to our spouses. Life together has a way of drawing out the best and worst in us. We become known. We become vulnerable. As the initial honeymoon glow wears off, we find ourselves living with a human being, not an angel. We may begin to feel as if we married a stranger. And indeed we may have if we've followed the American pattern of romance that seems built more on heat than light!

As we move into the day-to-day realities of marriage, we have opportunities to move beyond romance to intimacy, beyond cardiovascular palpitations to deep caring and loving. It all depends on our willingness to work toward acceptance of each other with our foibles, fallacies, and faults. Acceptance and affirmation allow intimacy to blossom. Criticism and rejection lead to the desert land of loneliness. There is probably nothing so sad as the sight of a couple living together defensively and in isolation from each other, unable to be vulnerable because of the hurt of rejection.

How do spouses communicate rejection to each other? We can't possibly consider all the ways, but there are several common expressions. First, and perhaps most devastating, is through *infidelity*. Partners who violate their marriage vows and enter into adultery, secretly or openly, strike at the heart of their union. Infidelity says to the spouse, "You're not good enough. You don't meet my needs." Most extramarital affairs are conducted secretly. Though the faithful spouse may not understand exactly what's happening, more often than not he senses that there is a reserve, a holding back, a closing off. The partner may seem distracted and strangely uninterested in either verbal or sexual communion. He may become more sensitive to criticism than normal, more defensive and even more argumentative.

Another way in which marriage partners show rejection is through *perfectionism*. This trait is usually rooted in a background of upbringing by strict parents who set very high goals and never seemed satisfied with the way their children were. They usually express very little affection and praise but are quick to point out faults and inconsistencies. Or, the parents may have been quick to criticize other people. Perhaps the regular Sunday roast featured the preacher. If we grow up with a steady diet of such criticism, we've probably learned to look for faults, demanding that other people live up to our idea of perfection. This is disastrous in a marriage. Nobody's perfect, and marriage proves it quickly if there was any doubt. I remember thinking, before I got married, that I really had things put together. I didn't see any sins in my life or areas where God needed to work. It didn't take very long after I got married to see how arrogant I'd been. At any rate, spouses who start focusing on things they don't like in their partner and who see their mates as rehabilitation projects are headed for serious trouble. That only brings out the worst in both spouses and creates disastrous divisions. Rejection (criticism) only invites rejection. Mutual criticism means misery and loneliness. For marriages to work there has to be a margin of tolerance. If you realize that you have as many faults as your spouse, from his point of view, this will help you to grant him the freedom to be himself. This doesn't mean partners can't communicate about areas that are bothering. By all means do. But by all means don't do it with an air of superiority and judgment, or a wedge will be driven and the relationship will crack. Perfectionism says to the partner, "You're not good enough — you must change before I can really love you." This creates an atmosphere of insecurity and drives the spouse into emotional hiding.

Third, spouses may show rejection by *not showing interest* in each other's lives. When we fail to ask questions and *listen* to our spouses, we run the risk of communicating that we don't think what they are doing is very important. Further, we indirectly may communicate that our partners aren't very important. If we don't take time to discuss our daily lives, our concerns, our anxieties, and our frustrations, we soon feel as though our spouses don't care. In the absence of showing interest, it's easy for one or both partners to feel they're being used and manipulated. Partners who have completely separate lives due to different interests, or separate living and working locations, have to work extra hard to bridge the gap.

Marriage partners may also communicate rejection, albeit unintentionally, in the way they make decisions and handle *conflicts*. Marital conflicts most often originate or are expressed when couples have to make decisions. The decisions may be as simple as where to put the new couch or as complex as how to cope with a handicapped baby or care for a widowed parent. The intensity and length of conflicts aren't directly related to the complexity of the decision. Couples can get into serious disagreements over the simplest matters — should the heat be turned down at night or the window opened, what color should the house be painted, or who should wash the car or mow the lawn, etc. Decisions need to be made daily. And there's no umpire to call balls and strikes. Partners often come to a decision with different values, needs, perceptions, and goals. These differences can become the basis for deeper intimacy and togetherness or lead to intense power struggles in which one or both partners feel put down and hurt. The biggest difficulties in most marital decision-making are usually the willingness to really hear out the partner's views, failure to adopt a problem-solving approach to the decision, a tendency to get off the issue and onto supposed hidden motives or blindnesses of the partner, and unwillingness to compromise. If decisions and conflicts are approached constructively, they provide opportunities for partners to express and clarify real feelings, to learn more about each other's values and goals, and to build each other's self-worth. If, however, they are battlegrounds (which they easily become if such a pattern develops early in marriage), we will find ourselves like armed enemies in splendid, horrible emotional isolation and loneliness. Usually it is the way the decisions and conflicts are conducted which gives feelings of rejection: stony silence or uncontrolled screaming don't readily convey a willingness to reason lovingly; insisting on always having one's own way makes a partner feel worthless; being unwilling to listen to one's partner denies both his importance and his very existence in the relationship. The list could go on almost indefinitely, but I'm sure the point is well made. Decisions and conflicts are opportunities for the growth or death of intimacy. They provide a garden of belonging or a gravel pit of emptiness.

6
MISSING
CONNECTIONS

It's hard to ignore five cats crawling around, under, and over you — especially when you have asthma. One of my childhood memories is of the visits our family made to various single or widowed older ladies. There were almost always the cats. I didn't understand then that pets help ease the pain of loneliness. Each animal had a name and "personality" of its own. The ladies talked to them, fussed over them, and treated them like people. The presence of these "people-pets" was comforting, I'm sure. Pets are important sources of affection and attachments for millions of people. They are companions who rarely reject us but draw out our caring and affection.

And yet pets don't completely remove the sting of loneliness. We need someone who answers when we talk. Many a lonely person draws great comfort simply from hearing a human voice. They turn the television or radio on just to feel as if someone else is around, even though they may not actually sit down and concentrate on the program. The popularity of talk shows comes in part from the need to be heard. We seem to have a built-in need to talk. If you don't believe me, try not talking *to anyone* for twenty-four hours. You'll probably start talking to yourself. Just being able to turn the television or radio on, even if we aren't really listening, helps avert or lessen feelings of loneliness.

But there's more. To simply talk or hear human voices isn't

enough in the long run. We need to talk about things that really matter and listen to others with sensitivity. The fundamental importance of dialogue is suggested in biblical descriptions of the beginning: "In the beginning was the Word, and the Word was with God, and the Word was God" (John 1:1). Christ the Word became the bridge between God and man. He crossed the chasm through His words and presence in human history. Words are bridges. They help us to reach across the great expanse from one individual to another. They draw us together. They give us entrance into the dreams, delights, and difficulties of each other. Words affirm us when they communicate understanding and acceptance by someone important to us. They help us to connect with each other.

Dialogue is the way to understanding. Understanding is built on reciprocal communication. It requires mutual give and take. Dialogue isn't always just words, either. As we discuss experiences and create a mutual history, we grow in our understanding of each other.

But words can also act like drawbridges. They can block others off from entering into our lives. They can be barriers to dialogue. They can hurt and reject and separate us. They can prevent or break the fragile bond of understanding which draws us out of our isolation and allows us to experience love.

Being understood communicates love. The absence of understanding ushers in loneliness. Without genuine dialogue and understanding, we don't enter into each other's souls and spirits. We stand alone and lonely, like Alice, who said, "I felt intensely lonely because of a personal matter I couldn't tell my closest friends. I really needed to tell someone, but I felt they wouldn't understand. I told them and they really didn't understand, even though they tried to. I felt so lonely."

Dialogue also involves progressive risk-taking and exposure of ourselves to another person. It allows gradually longer peeks behind our masks until there's less need to wear the mask with one's intimate(s). It must be mutual if it's to be a genuine connection, one that satisfies and affirms.

It's important to realize that no one will ever *completely* understand us. We're born alone and we die alone. We grow up with experiences that are different from those of anyone else. We are unique, and, as a result, it takes time to build bridges. Too many people give up when the bridge is only half-done. Bridge-building takes effort; there are problems that have to be solved before it can be completed. Many aren't willing to endure or to risk hurt. They see difficulties as insurmountable and the process as too lengthy. So they remain unknown, misunderstood, and lonely.

For those who stick around to see the bridge completed, there are the delights of belonging and being understood. There are the joys of intimacy and mutual affirmation. Loneliness disappears in the process of knowing and being known. As one psychologist put it, "Nothing thaws loneliness more quickly than understanding."[1]

Unfortunately, our picture of bridge-building isn't completely accurate. We never completely understand each other because dialogue is a process. Rather, we build bridges from one island of understanding to another. Building intimacy is a lifetime process because life itself is a process. Our past continually interacts with our present in ways that can't be completely predicted.

There are several factors which hinder or prevent dialogue and promote loneliness. These are *physical isolation*, *role isolation*, and *social isolation*.

Physical isolation hinders dialogue because it prevents the isolated person from regularly relating to others. It results in a lack of shared meanings. Establishing meaningful, intimate communication requires people to spend time together and to share experiences. Kids living in neighborhoods with few other kids their age feel isolated. So do people who live in the country. Homes are far apart; besides church and an occasional grange meeting, there's often very little opportunity to meet and get to know others.

Those who are without transportation frequently find it difficult to make or maintain friendships. As a result of urbanization, friends and family may live several miles apart, even when they're in the same city. Many elderly people have to give up driving and may not be able to catch buses to see their friends. They may find themselves alone most of the time, with hardly anyone who can or does make the effort to see them or take them to church and other social activities. When someone finally does visit them, the visitor may find himself barraged by talk. Due to physical isolation, the "cut-off" person stores up things to talk about. Unfortunately, the result is often more monologue than dialogue and drives people away.

People who are confined to hospitals or nursing homes are also likely to experience loneliness due to physical isolation. Though there are others around them in the hospital or home, most are sick and centered on themselves. Many have given up on life and don't care to make friendships. Others are so sick they can't. Placement in a home or hospital removes people from their social networks — their work buddies, neighborhood friends, or church acquaintances. They are out of the mainstream. Because of this, friends who are physically able to come and visit do so infrequently; they are busy with their own life situations and usually find it difficult to break away for regular visits.

The telephone is a help, of course. But it doesn't allow full dialogue because it is at least partially public. It costs money for long distance calls (and it's awfully hard to get into a meaningful conversation in three minutes), and it doesn't allow you to receive and interpret nonverbal language. Voice tone and intensity alone may be confusing and misinterpreted. Real dialogue requires in-the-flesh experiences. A hug, kiss, touch, and smile are awfully tough to communicate over a phone, but they're vital nonverbal signs of affirmation.

People in leadership positions are sometimes unable to enter into authentic dialogue with others because of *role isolation*. Often they are unable to express what they're really feeling because of external expectations that are put upon them by others. The speaking that leaders do may also have added meanings attached. Their every word, facial expression, and intonation may be closely scrutinized. This is because how they speak and feel has significant impact upon the lives of those dependent upon them. This, coupled with a sense of having to be invulnerable heroes, and of competitiveness with other leaders who may be after their position, often leads to loneliness.

Pastors are especially expected to be emotionally self-sufficient and invulnerable to feelings of doubt and discouragement. They are to be strong and invincible, not given to any weakness. They are to always understand others and to accept being misunderstood as a hazard of their position. Because of these unwritten role expectations, pastors are normally unable to enter into genuine dialogue with those in their congregations. They are emotionally isolated because of their role. Often this emphasis on image results in messages which are doctrinally correct and exhortationally powerful, but which leave members feeling discouraged. This is because the pastor doesn't reveal any personal understanding of the struggles and realities of trying to put the message into practice. Because of congregational expectations, he is unable to identify with weakness and so fails to speak on the level of emotional reality. Even more tragic is the reality that pastors often can't even unburden themselves genuinely with other pastors. There is the fear of rejection, of being seen as a spiritual pygmy among spiritual giants. The result is that many pastors struggle with depression and feelings of isolation. They have to constantly play the role of the perfectionist.

A good example of such isolation, [John] is a middle-aged pastor who described himself as a loner all his life. His wife agreed that he allowed no one to know him intimately, including her. Presenting himself as a self-reliant perfectionist, an image designed to intimidate everyone he met, he confessed that inside he was scared and insecure but afraid to let anyone know it. He was terrified that they might not accept him if he wasn't perfect. . . . For John, the moment of truth came as his marriage relationship began to deteriorate.[2]

Other leaders find themselves similarly isolated and misunderstood. They may have to undertake painful actions such as firing employees and then endure the wrath of people who don't understand because they lack information. They may be unable to voice deep concerns related to their leadership because of possible leaks, potential crises of confidence which might result from the simple act of talking, or distortions of the meaning and impact of what concerns them.

As we've already suggested in an earlier chapter, the life of a celebrity is also often lonely because people usually relate to them only as role performers. Speaking about the lonely side of being a celebrity, Elisabeth Kübler-Ross revealed:

You are adored and put on a pedestal, but you have dinner alone and breakfast alone. It's a terrible loneliness. And people treat you like a demi-god. All you want is for somebody to say, "Come and have a cup of coffee with me and take your shoes off." You know — be a normal human being. . . . But you don't have any of that — people treat you like you're not human.[3]

Some people find themselves cut off from dialogue and lonely because they are *out* of a role. This is especially true for newly retired people. Retirees have lost the close association of people they've been used to relating to. Unless they are able to carry on those friendships outside of their work, they find themselves cut off from people who have shared their goals, time, and even their language (most professors, for example, have a specialized language that those outside the profession don't readily understand). Many retirees not only lose friends, but they also lose purpose and meaning. They find themselves wondering who they are and what their new life should be. Frequently this results in a period of depression while adjustments are made. A key to overcoming depression and loneliness is the extent to which the retiree's spouse can gently and consistently show understanding, as well as listen and encourage his or her spouse in new directions. This is not easy, either, for retirement normally brings major adjustments for both spouses. As they are able to express their frustrations, anger, and hopes to each other without feeling rejected, they will find new levels of depth and enjoyment emerging. Retirees need to cultivate outside interests long before retirement to ease adjustments.

Perhaps one of the most common but least wise things for new retirees to do is to move to a new location far from family and friends. Many will move several hundred or thousand miles to their retirement dream land. Initially this will only intensify adjustments to retirement. Unless there are abundant opportunities for meeting new people and the retirees are socially outgoing, such a major move will most likely promote loneliness rather than happiness. It rips them out of their former framework of friends and leaves them only with each other. Often they become strangers because of the new roles and identities they must forge.

A third major cause of breakdown in dialogue is due to *social isolation*. Shyness and misunderstanding cause large numbers of people to feel separated from each other.

Psychologist Phil Zimbardo suggests that *shyness* is like a psychological prison. Over 40 percent of people that he surveyed felt that they were shy at that point in time, and 80 percent had been shy sometime.[4] Fewer than 20 percent of those answering Zimbardo's survey did not label themselves as shy. About a third of the respondents felt shy about 50 percent of the time. We have consistently found that shy people are more lonely. This is probably because shyness involves both some degree of anxiety and social awkwardness in the presence of other people. For most this is felt only in some situations or with some people. For others, interaction with anyone is painful and terrifying. They find it difficult to meet the eyes of others; speaking to anyone is very difficult; people are avoided. Many shy people lack appropriate social skills.

Tom sneaks into the back pew of the church and leaves while the pastor is saying the benediction. He is afraid to talk in any group and only talks one-to-one, when he is concerned. He doesn't meet anyone's eyes straight on. One gets the impression that Tom is terribly anxious about receiving approval, so much so that he avoids people and the possibility that he might be disapproved.

Extremely shy people are highly self-conscious. They lack confidence in themselves and constantly worry about being rejected. Publicly they are quiet, but privately their heads whirl with thoughts. They are preoccupied with themselves — how they look, what kind of impression they're making, or what others will think. The result is that they are often socially awkward because they're not paying attention to the cues given by others which help regulate social interaction. They are so busy with their inner thoughts that they leave those around them uncertain about how to act. This raises the cost of relating by the others and tends to drive them away. Shyness, then, results in social problems, depression, loneliness, difficulty in appropriately asserting opinions and values, poor self-projection (people misread what he's like), and difficulty in communicating clearly.

Shy people believe that *they* are the cause of their shyness — it's part of who they are. Shyness seems to be learned. It can come from a history of being put down by others, learning to be incompetent in order to gain attention, listening passively to large amounts of television, or learning to put oneself down in front of others. Shyness may also be encouraged by the high levels of moving in our society, which make it necessary to break into a new group with each move.

Shyness acts as a barrier to intimacy because it exaggerates the need for ''safety.'' Shy people find it more difficult to risk the exposure of themselves that intimacy requires. Allowing themselves to be known is emotionally overwhelming. Some turn to impersonal sex, alcohol, or violence in desperate attempts to make some kind of intimate connection with another living person.

Shyness, then, separates people because of the fear of rejection. One result of shyness is intense loneliness due to their inability to establish relationships with emotional depth. Close relationships are risky because they require vulnerability and self-disclosure. Without vulnerability and mutual disclosure there can be no intimacy. Where fear dominates, loneliness thrives.

Some of our loneliest moments are when we feel that the people who count in our lives *don't understand* us. Psychologists have found, for example, that young men who described their fathers as not at all understanding when they were kids felt very lonely, frustrated, and unimportant when they approached their dads. They usually thought their dad's minds were somewhere else when they tried to communicate.

Dialogue, or communication, is a complex, two-way process. It involves a minimum of two people, each of whom acts both as a sender and a receiver (see Figure 1).

MESSAGE FILTERS

SENDER	RELATIONSHIP TO EACH OTHER	
1. Background	1. Past interaction	
2. Emotional state	2. Current relationship	
3. Personality	3. Role expectations	
4. Intentions	4. Difference in values	
5. Appearance		
	RECEIVER	MESSAGE RECEIVED (Interpreted)
	1. Personality	
	2. Interpersonal sensitivity	
	3. Background	
MESSAGE SENT	4. Assumptions	
1. Verbal	5. Physical and emotional state	
2. Nonverbal	6. Selective listening	
	SITUATION	
	1. What's expected?	
	2. Other people present?	

Figure 1
The Communication Process

In the actual process of dialogue we jump back and forth in those roles. There are six messages which can come through in the process of dialogue:

1. What you mean to say.
2. What you actually say.
3. What the other person hears.
4. What the other person thinks he hears.
5. What the other person says about what you said.
6. What you think the other person said about what you said.[5]

It's obviously easy for a breakdown in communication to occur with all of these possible interpretations.

Let's take a closer look at the communication process. Figure 1 shows the major ingredients. Misunderstanding can arise at almost any point in the process.

First, when we try to communicate with another person our personal history, current emotions, personality, and intentions all affect the way we send our message and how it's received. For example, if we have come from a background where money was scarce, the way that we talk about our spouse's overcharges on the charge accounts is liable to be more pointed and intense than otherwise. Our spouse's actions and intentions may be misinterpreted and our communication more hostile because we're really communicating through our background. Similar backgrounds give a better basis for understanding.

Whether we're happy, contented, angry, or anxious will affect *what* we say and *how* we say it, especially in more private, intimate communication. Messages delivered in anger are often misperceived by the receiver; the tone of anger triggers defensiveness and more easily results in misunderstanding. We're also less tuned to our partner's perceptions and feelings when we're feeling mad. Other feelings usually influence our communications indirectly, through nonverbal channels. They often cause misunderstanding because they can be interpreted in several ways.

People with introverted personalities communicate differently than extroverts; their relative passiveness and quietness may lead receivers to discount the value of their communication. Even things an introvert or shy person feels deeply about may not come out that way, because their delivery of the message isn't assertive or intense enough. Those with low self-esteem find it more difficult to trust others and present themselves less attractively than those with higher self-esteem. They expect social failure and tend to prompt it by presenting themselves negatively. They also tend to personalize and bend messages in relation to themselves and have more difficulty being objective.

If our intentions are positive, it is more likely that we will deliver our message candidly and honestly than if we're trying to communicate with intentions that aren't apparent or positive. One of the reasons parents often seem nonunderstanding to teens is that they try to discern the intentions behind the teenager's request. Teens often see what the parents intend to be concern as unreasonable, distrustful, controlling, and intrusive. At the same time, parents misread the teens and use their cries for independence as rejection.

Finally, appearance plays a part in how our messages are received. People who are well-dressed, better looking, and smile are more likely to have their messages positively received than a sloppily dressed, homely, and frowning communicator. I learned this lesson several years ago when I worked part-time as a parking lot attendant. People going to three different events used the lot, so we had certain places set aside for each kind of patron. One thing that became quite apparent was that a lot of people felt they had the right to park their gleaming ''boats'' anywhere they chose, and no grubby, low-class, attendant was going to tell them where to park. After numerous skirmishes I decided to try an experiment. I dressed up in a sport coat, slacks, and tie and performed with all the class I could muster up. Would you believe that everybody did what I asked, with no arguments?

When we relate to others we communicate on two levels — the verbal and the nonverbal. As relationships develop, considerable weight is put upon our nonverbal message. That's because we usually assume nonverbal expressions are harder to manage or control and are more honest. There's an old saying — "What you do speaks more loudly than what you say" — which seems to be true. The greatest likelihood of misunderstanding comes when there's an apparent conflict between our words and our nonverbal messages. "I love you" can be said questioningly, flatly, or passionately. If a person says "I love you" but won't help us in times of need, we'll probably question his sincerity. Behavior, facial expressions, body posture, gestures, loudness and intensity of voice, crying, laughing, and eye glance all communicate meanings. For example, missionaries often get into the embarrassing predicament of using a wrong word or intonation. Depending on the word and the hearers, this will be amusing or threatening. Tom Stebbins, former missionary to South Vietnam, tells about the confusion which can arise when the wrong tone is used. In South Vietnam there are five tones. The same basic word *ma* can mean mother, rice, shoot, horse, or devil depending on the intonation! Diplomats and heads of state must carefully weigh their words and nonverbal cues to make sure they're conveying the right (intended) meanings to their hearers.

Often very similar nonverbal expressions carry very different meanings — they are dependent upon the context or situation we're in. The result is that there's a good chance of misunderstanding. Sometimes we intentionally mix messages — we may want to say something negatively but are afraid to, so we speak positive words but give negative nonverbal cues. At other times we mix messages unintentionally — our backgrounds or emotional states may influence us, though we don't realize it. For example, a man may respond with impatience, not because he's impatient with the person he's talking to, but because he broke up with his girlfriend the night before and feels irritable.

Misunderstanding also results when the wrong words are used. In close relationships, we learn that certain words or phrases delight our partners, while others are calls to battle. This is due to our partner's past. Words are "wrong" when they stir up meanings in our partner's mind that we didn't intend, or when they make our partner feel put down. Carefully chosen words are especially crucial when people talk about "sensitive" areas or try to correct or disagree with someone. Unless they're the right words spoken in a manner that is received as caring, they are likely to communicate rejection, whether or not we intended it.

To connect with our partner, we have to shape our communications with him or her in mind. Usually we focus more on what we want to say than on how it will be received. Therein lies the root of much misunderstanding. Judd Swihart, in his little book *How Do You Say, I Love You?*, points out the trouble that occurs in marriages when partners choose different "languages" of love. For example, the husband may feel that providing a beautiful home and lots of money is communicating love, while the wife focuses on the time he is working and away from her as indications that he doesn't love her. These languages are learned while growing up and exert tremendous influence on a couple's relationship. Unless partners can get beyond disagreement and begin to make clear their respective love-languages, they will get locked into a cycle of misunderstanding that will leave each feeling used, unloved, and lonely. Partners must take time to explore and clarify what communicates love and what doesn't. Swihart argues that each of us has an identifiable primary "language" which we hear as acceptance and love.

The relationship that two people have significantly affects how communication is conducted. If past interaction has been stormy, affirmation and understanding are more difficult. Previous reliability affects willingness to communicate about deeply personal matters. For example, 40 percent of college-age adults and 33 percent of 15 to 17 year olds feel they don't have a single friend they can rely on. Like it or not, we carry memories into our relationships — they either help or hinder us. This is why forgiveness is so important — without it, hurts dominate our memories and destroy dialogue. People are usually attracted to one another because they share central interests, values, or goals. Sometimes as relationships deepen, partners feel alienated because they discover that their guiding values are not the same as they had once thought.

Communication is filtered by the receiver so that the message which is finally heard is affected by the receiver's thoughts and feelings, as well as by the sender-receiver relationship and the situation in which the dialogue occurs.

The receiver's background and personality may cause him to distort the message. For example, people who have been raised by very critical parents will hear and respond more to comments or expressions which might be interpreted as criticism. People with very low self-esteem find it difficult to accept positive comments, and yet they seem to crave such expressions and feel rejected if they're not regularly reassured. Some people are more interpersonally sensitive than others and can read "messages" of need more readily than others. My wife is like this and is able to respond with care and concern much more quickly than many others. As a result, she is quickly sought out by people — they feel she really understands and cares about them (which she does).

Sometimes misunderstanding arises because of the assumption that the receiver makes. One of the biggest complaints in marriages is that the partner doesn't really listen or understand. Many teens feel similarly about their parents. This is because most of us assume that we know what our partner is going to say — especially if we've known them for a while — and concentrate on what *we're* going to say rather than on listening. Genuine listening gently probes, asks questions, and moves toward understanding. We must be careful not to answer before we hear, because the assumptions we make may be wrong.

Receivers will hear things differently depending on their

physical and emotional state. Generally speaking, it's much better to get into "heavy" discussions when we're physically fresh. Arguments and misunderstandings increase with tiredness. Married couples would do better to save such matters until morning time, if possible, unless they're both "night owls." It's also important to understand that how we feel emotionally colors what we hear. If we're depressed, we're more likely to hear things which affirm our depression. Part of the key to successful communication is knowing *when* to communicate as well as how. Our physical and emotional condition causes us to selectively listen and will either increase or decrease understanding. There is some indication that the biological changes which occur during puberty increase teens' sensitivity to rejection, as well as create instability in their relationships due to drastic mood swings. Part of growing through adolescence is learning how to get in touch with one's often explosive feelings and moderate them so they don't drive one into unwise relationships or away from parents.

Finally, our dialogue and interpretations are always set in a context. Whether an act or words are public or private, expected or unexpected, affects our response. I have seen people register deep hurt when a partner has made derogatory comments in public — always in jest, of course. Such public communication only humiliates the partner and drives the two apart in private. Generally speaking, unexpected words or behaviors carry greater significance than the expected. An "I love you" card, surprise note, flowers, or invitation to dinner that doesn't fall on a holiday, birthday, or anniversary may speak volumes more than meeting the expected, commercial traditions.

Too many marriages are marked by lonely partners who don't feel understood. Usually they've given up trying to communicate about things that matter. They've allowed past misunderstandings to turn them into pessimists. Because they're not stretching out to touch each other, they shrink into silent isolation.

Too many teens also feel misunderstood. They want to share their inner feelings, express their own ideas. But so many feel that what they have to say doesn't matter or will be dismissed by their parents. Too many parents feel misunderstood and maligned by the children they've poured themselves out for.

Not feeling understood *is* one of the key dimensions of loneliness. Being understood takes work. It requires dialogue that cuts through the conscious and unconscious distortions which so easily beset communication. It takes courage to allow ourselves to be known and to share our inner feelings. It takes a willingness to spend time together, sharing thoughts and experiences. Without dialogue and understanding there is loneliness.

A *Special Word about Singles*

In our society, singles have frequently felt both that they don't really belong and that no one really understands them. Until recently, to be single was to feel like a misfit. There was no "nice" place to go to enjoy other singles without being in a dating situation. Churches seldom had any special programs for singles. Couples had their own sets of friends, so singles normally felt like a fifth wheel in married circles.

Some of this continues. Even today most churches don't have any special groups or programs which recognize the special friendship needs of singles. Many of the secular meeting places foster fornication rather than friendship. But things are changing. There are singles groups in churches and apartment complexes for singles which take social needs into account. There are at least a couple of reasons for the change.

People are marrying later. From 1970-78, the median age was delayed a full year (24.2 for men, 21.8 for women). This is partly due to the more permissive ethic of cohabitation. Over 1.1 million unmarried couples, more than double the number in 1970, lived together in 1978. Many of these people eventually end up marrying. In addition to these "nonsingle singles," however, many people are either delaying marriage or choosing the single life. In 1978, 48 percent of women in their early twenties had never married, compared to 28 percent in 1960. The number of women living alone is up 42 percent since 1970. This amounts to 10.4 million. In addition, the number of men living alone has risen 79 percent, to 6.4 million. That amounts to almost 17 million adults who live alone. About 40 percent of these are over 65.

Several studies consistently report that between three and four times as many singles suffer from loneliness as marrieds. Younger adults generally report that being unattached makes them feel lonely. Their longing tends to be more general, not specifically focused on a person, as in the case of widows. Usually loneliness among elderly singles is more related to forced isolation due to being hospitalized.

Among never married younger adults, there are several things which feed into loneliness. If the single decides to live alone, he is faced with an *empty apartment*. As wonderful as this may sound at times to beleagured parents of young children, it wears thin quickly. Simply being alone causes loneliness. This is especially true at meal times, when returning to the apartment after work or an evening out, on weekends, and over holidays. There's no one to talk with, and you just can't call people you know and say, "Can I come over tonight? I feel lonely. I need someone to talk to!" When things go wrong at work, when somebody has been unfair or misunderstands, there's no one to talk to. There's no one to clarify, to understand, on a daily basis. Relationships may be available, but they often have to be scheduled. This introduces formality and makes it harder for free and deep intimacy.

Some singles live with a roommate. If the partner has been chosen primarily for financial reasons, to share the rent, what frequently results is two people sharing space but not themselves. They're really business partners, not friends. Unless the roommates are friends to begin with, there may not be either compatibility or even the willingness to work at a personal relationship. Each may have his own set of friends. Fortunately, some singles are able to live with friends. Even this has difficulties, however, because inevitably there will be adjustments required — when and what to watch on television, what time to get up, should clothes be shared, should food be bought and prepared jointly or separately, and so forth. If roommates aren't equally committed to the relationship, such adjustments will result in conflicts. Sooner or later one will move out, and both will feel even more lonely than before. Except for the additional unifying influences of sexual intimacy and legal constraints, living with a friend is much like living with a spouse.

Frustrated sexual needs may also lead to intense loneliness. Those who try to relieve their needs through masturbation often feel guilty and unworthy. Their activities may make them feel isolated from God. They may also feel that they can't let themselves be fully known to others because of this secret sin. If masturbation becomes obsessive, it may further hinder development of appropriate close relationships because of the focus on sex and fantasy that it involves. Some will choose to become ''sexually active'' and engage in transient sexual relationships. These inevitably alienate the participants from each other except for the brief moments of actual intercourse. Sex without commitment saddens and separates. In addition to the emotional dissatisfaction and emptiness of such relationships, there is the guilt of violating God's moral law. This is especially true for the Christian, of course, or for those with similar ethical standards. Others will more satisfactorily meet their sexual needs as they attach themselves to purposes and people that allow expression and receipt of affection, including appropriate forms of nonsexual touching.

Part of the loneliness of singles comes from *feelings of failure*. Our society has programmed us to believe that if we're normal adults we'll be married. From their earliest years, girls are taught to plan for marriage. They play at it, think about it, and hope for the magic moment. Boys aren't quite so well-trained; it's just assumed they'll get married. By the time a gal reaches 25 or a guy 28 to 30, parents and relatives often start making noises about how nice it would be to have grandkids and nephews. Well-meaning friends (usually married couples) take to trying to arrange matches, and the pressure is on. Simple comparison with brothers, sisters, and friends who are married and having children is enough to throw some women into deep depression. Especially in women there seems to be a deep need to have children that becomes increasingly intense during the 30s. This leads to despair and loneliness until the reality of lifelong singleness is accepted and alternatives can be found. Singles at this point can be delightful aunts and uncles *if* they don't push themselves too boldly into the families of their siblings.

Some singles also are lonely because of *misconceptions about marriage*. They're exposed to unbridled romanticism on every hand. The idea is that the handsome prince finds his Cinderella, and the charming miss marries her conquering hero. In both cases they ride off on a white steed to live happily ever after in marital bliss. Somebody ought to let singles in on the secret. More often he and she ride off in a dented pumpkin that isn't paid for, the prince seems more like a frog, and the miss is more alarming than charming. Good marriages are wonderful. They *do* bring deep satisfaction. They *are* places of belonging and acceptance. But they don't just happen. They require work and faith and adjustments and prayer, and even some hurt. They're marked by downs as well as ups and misunderstanding as well as intimacy. Marriage is not instant bliss, a paradise of sexual ecstasy, or a garden of total acceptance and happiness. It has all of those elements to be sure, but it's not what our imagination sometimes cooks up when we're on the outside wishing in.

Preliminary feelings of loneliness in young singles may also prompt orientations which lead to even greater loneliness in the long run. One trap is to become centered on *material acquisitions*. Because of fewer obligations and in spite of certain tax

and lending policies that seem to be antisingle, singles are freer
to spend money on things. Things can become their family,
treasured like a spouse and children. Things, however, can never
replace people. Acquisitions may help us feel more successful,
by comparison, but they don't bring the deep satisfaction of
communion. Singles need to build friendships of both sexes that
will bring comfort and companionship. Indeed, the absence of
those who care (normally family but it *can* be close friends) is
what makes the elderly years difficult for many never married
singles. Without family and seasoned friends in the last years,
we can only feel worthless and lonely. Things will never bring us
the satisfaction we need when we're growing older.

Another part of single experience that prompts loneliness is
the emphasis on family and belonging that goes with major
holidays such as Thanksgiving and Christmas. Unless the single
has developed special traditions of his own with others, or ''is
adopted'' by a family, holidays can be emotionally bleak.
Although it is probably impossible to completely erase loneliness for people who are single or otherwise separated from loved
ones during these special ''belonging times,'' there are a couple
of practical strategies that help. First, involve other people. If
you have been developing friendships with other people who are
in a similar situation during the rest of the year, it will be easy for
you to invite them to spend the holiday with you, and much more
satisfying than just picking someone at random. Take the initiative and don't passively wait for someone to invite you. Second,
develop your own traditions. One group I know has been getting
together for New Year's Day for about seven years to watch
football, snack and talk together, put puzzles together, and
simply have a good time. They're mostly singles. Perhaps there
are community events, including cantatas, which regularly happen at holidays, that can become part of your holiday calendar.
Third, reach out. What an excellent time holidays are for touching others in need. Perhaps you can visit rest homes, a children's
hospital, or a home for the disabled and bring cheer to those in

even less desirable circumstances. If all else fails, you may wish to volunteer to work if someone is needed at your place of employment.

Having said all of this, I don't wish to leave the impression that being single is necessarily a time of despair. Many singles find deep satisfaction in their jobs, friends, and freedom. As they learn to give of themselves in creative ways to those around them, they find that loneliness is only an occasional visitor rather than a constant companion.

7
LOVING AND LOSING

Can you imagine a world where you would never have to be separated from the ones you love? It sounds a bit like heaven, doesn't it? Here on earth, separation is an unavoidable part of life. We move, leave home, break dating relationships, get divorced, and die. Each separation carries feelings of anxiety, grief, and loneliness. The loss of a close relationship is probably more lonely than the failure to gain it in the first place.

In this chapter we'll look at some of the common separation events that bring loneliness into our lives. The loneliness of loss is perhaps even more painful than being misunderstood or not belonging. When we lose a relationship we lose part of ourselves — the time, energy, commitment, feelings, and memories which we have given to a loved one. Some loss events don't mean a total loss of attachment, though they may feel like it. Some of the broken bonds are permanent, such as through death. In each case, however, we experience a very real sense of abandonment. There is a common experience of anxiety, anger, searching for the lost loved one, grief, and loneliness that each of these events ushers in.

First Connections

If you're a parent, you've probably experienced it. There you

126

were, trying to get to a special event on time, and your little fourteen month old was filling the air with screams and sobs. He didn't want to be separated from you. All the convincing rhetoric in the world probably didn't turn your little one's beet red face back to its normal color. It seems as if your child didn't understand, or didn't believe, that you were really coming back. Frustrating for you, frightening for him.

In that kind of situation, it's easy to think your child is spoiled. But that's probably not the case. Rather, he is feeling *separation anxiety*. He is afraid that you might not return and is overwhelmed by a sense of possible loss. Separation anxiety tells us that the infant has formed an important attachment with his parents. Although it normally appears toward the end of the first year, the first signs may appear as early as three months, when an infant cries solely to be picked up and held.

Attachment begins to develop in the first few weeks after birth. As early as the second month, babies pay special attention to their mothers. They selectively smile, cry, coo, follow with their eyes, and turn toward their mother. She is able to comfort her baby when no one else can. By about the sixth month a unique attachment is formed. Even the attachment a baby forms with its father is different. Children appear to be equally attached to mother and father by the first year, *until* they're faced with the need for comfort. When a stranger appears, for example, babies immediately try to get close to their mothers. This may be due to the way that most fathers act toward babies; fathers usually don't touch the child as frequently, and they speak in more adultlike language.

Between eight and twelve months, stranger anxiety appears. The infant has formed a mental image of mother that is based on familiarity. A stranger's face doesn't match the baby's image and is frightening. A baby usually responds with caution or avoidance or fright when a stranger tries to come close. This is sometimes embarrassing when the "stranger" is Great Aunt Matilda who sent the baby an elaborate gift. But it's simply the infant's way of assuring its own protection. Infants who form a secure bond with their mothers are more secure and trusting than those who don't, as they grow older. The quality of early mother-child attachment is crucial if a child is to later form similar attachments with others. Institutionalized children who are socially mistreated or ignored during their first year have greater difficulty forming long-term attachments, are more impulsive and aggressive, and lack confidence in themselves. This is true even when they receive subsequent mothering and family care.[1]

Long-term separation from a mother during the second or third year seems to have a severe impact on the child's ability to form close relationships in later life.[2] Also, early parental loss can lead to severe adult depression, antisocial behavior, neurosis, suicide, and psychosis.[3] This and low self-esteem are most likely to promote chronic loneliness. At first, children respond to separation with protest — screaming, crying, wildly running around. Crying and screaming are especially prevalent at bedtime. The children actively search for their mothers. Then they seem to display despair. They are constantly preoccupied with their mothers and express deep resentment and rage toward their mothers for abandoning them. After several months the children apparently forget their mothers and are able to relate to peers and adults. If the mother returns after a period of separation, the child may turn away or try to get away from her. If the separation hasn't been too long, she will gradually be able to restore the attachment. Often, however, the child clings in a highly dependent and annoying way which may cause friction between mother and child. The child's clinging is simply a nonverbal way to insure that mommy won't go away again.

By the end of the third year, most children are able to tolerate temporary separation from their mothers with little anxiety. Based on the security of their bond with mother, they are able to build other close relationships with peers and parent-substitutes. The two most prevalent causes of permanent separation between parents and children are death and divorce. While death rates for adults under forty-four have declined, divorce rates have skyrocketed during this century. There is now one divorce for every 1.8 marriages in the U.S. About 57 percent of divorces obtained in 1976 involved children. Over one million children have been involved in divorce proceedings each year since 1972. About 30 percent of the kids growing up in the 1970s will go through the divorce of their parents.

Since 1970 the divorce rate has continued to climb while the rate of remarriage has sharply dropped. This means that only about one third of U.S. households are made up of both parents and their children. In fact, single-parent families are increasing about twenty times faster than two-parent families.[4] In 1979, there were almost 4.9 million single-parent households. In addition to climbing divorce rates, illegitimate birth rates have climbed sharply from 3.9 percent of all live births in 1950 to 14.2 percent in 1975. Many of these children will never know their fathers. The combined result of divorce, illegitimate births, and death means that about 50 percent of the children born in the '80s will live in a single-parent family for a significant portion of their childhood.

What effects will this have? Probably the best indicator of the impact of divorce or death on children is the mother's response. The mother's psychological state affects her kids' mental health. The drop in remarriages may not be all bad, as some studies show that there are greater difficulties in adjusting to divorce when a mother remarries. Adjustment to divorce seems related to a child's age.[5] Preschoolers show the most deterioration in their behavior; they tend to blame themselves for the divorce and also have difficulty expressing their feelings. Kids that are seven or eight are more able to express their sadness and don't blame themselves for the divorce. They do tend to have strong feelings of rejection and abandonment. Nine and ten year olds also feel rejected and experience loneliness, mainly due to neglect by parents wrapped up in their marital wars. These kids are able to acknowledge anger as well as sadness. Adolescents generally display very articulate and intense feelings of anger, loss, depression, shame, and embarrassment. They struggle with worry about *their* own ability to maintain a marriage relationship in the future.

More than death, divorce appears to increase a person's vulnerability in later life. This is somewhat surprising. Nevertheless, the younger a person is at the time when his parents divorce, the more lonely and self-rejecting he is as an adult.[6] The most lonely adults are those whose parents died before they were six years of age. Adult loneliness consistently decreases with increased age at the time of the parents' divorce (up to age eighteen). Those whose parents die during childhood do not seem to differ in adult loneliness or lowered self-esteem from those whose parents were alive throughout childhood.

Adults who before they were eighteen saw their parents divorce experience more crying spells, constant worry, irrational fears, feelings of worthlessness, guilt-feelings, trouble concentrating, and hopelessness, among other things, than those whose parents aren't divorced. Adults who were children when their parents divorced report feeling more anxious, afraid, and angry when they were alone than those with intact families. This fits the separation anxiety picture that we presented earlier.

Why is divorce more apt to lead to chronic loneliness than death? Shaver and Rubinstein suggest several reasons.[7] First, divorce is usually more gradual and is usually preceded by conflict. Children may try to intervene, be ignored or rebuffed, and end up feeling both helpless and rejected. Second, the parent the child stays with is likely to say negative things about the absent parent. This may create uncertainty and anxiety about the (usually) father's love. Third, under the stresses of single parenthood, the mother may have moments of frustration when the child is made to feel unwanted.

Day Care

Can someone else take the place of a mother without hurting

the child emotionally and socially? This is an important issue in modern America. Due to divorces and economic stress, almost 50 percent of U.S. wives are now employed, compared to 20 percent just thirty years ago. The Urban Institute estimates that 75 percent will be working by 1990. In 1977, husbands and wives from 8 million families *both* held year-round, full-time jobs. More than 5.6 million mothers with children under six worked in 1976. At least 2 million kids between ages three and thirteen have to care for themselves because mother works; 200,000 are between three and six years old. In 1978 8 million families were supported by women not living with a husband.

Can day care centers fill the need? Several cross-cultural studies suggest that multiple mothering *within the home* did not hurt children and may actually help children from poorer homes.[8] But what about multiple-mothering *outside* the home? At this point it appears that there are no significant differences in attachment when groups of day care children are compared with home-reared kids. *However*, it is important to point out that this conclusion has several important limitations. First, the day care facilities studied were staffed by highly competent workers and had a low child-to-adult ratio (3-1). This is highly unusual. Second, the children were all from intact families. Third, the children were each given a primary caretaker who played with them one or two hours each day. Also, the curriculum was oriented toward cognitive development and provided for much one-to-one social interaction between caretaker and child.[9] Finally, the results are given for groups, not individuals.

These findings point out the importance of quality interaction between a specific adult and child. Children from deprived homes may benefit both emotionally and socially. At the same time, it seems as though the cards were stacked. The very fact that normal home-rearing did not differ from a carefully controlled and enriched day care setting tells us that home-rearing by the mother is generally the best option. In most day care centers there is not sufficient staff or creativity to promote the kind of healthy emotional, mental, and social development that was found in this study. Also, we simply don't have enough research to tell us exactly what day care conditions promote healthy relationships *over the long run*.

If both parents absolutely need to work during their children's preschool years, it is probably best to place the children in a private home with a single caretaker and only two or three other children present. This will provide much more consistent and personalized care than most day care centers. Even this arrangement has difficulties, however. The child will spend more time with the paid caretaker than with the mother and may become more attached to the caretaker. The child doesn't know any better and couldn't help it if he did. Some of the delightful moments of development which draw mother and child together, such as first steps and first words, will also belong to the caretaker. It is likely that the caretaker will still not give the same amount and quality of attention and care as the mother would. (Obviously, I'm talking here about good mothers who would spend time caring for their kids if they were home.) Usually the caretaker's own children come first. If she has no children of her own, she may not be as adept as the mother, either. Finally, the caretaker may move, leaving the child feeling abandoned and neglected.

Modern Nomads

Each day more than one hundred thousand Americans change residences. Between 1970 and 1975 almost half the people in America moved. It has been estimated that the average American will move at least fourteen times in his lifetime. In one recent year, more Americans changed residences than the combined populations of Cambodia, Ghana, Guatemala, Iraq, Israel, Mongolia, Nicaragua, and Tunisia![10] It now takes an average of twenty years for a person to go from manager to president of a company. This process involves about seven geographical moves and eleven positional ones.[11]

We're definitely a people on the move. But what are we gaining with all our moving? Bigger and newer houses, job advancements, a change of scenery, new friends — true. We're also reaping a bumper crop of loneliness. Any move, especially if more than thirty miles, destroys a complex network of old relationships. The nomads of the past, such as Abraham when he left Ur, carried their physical and social belongings with them. The whole family and rest of the tribe usually went. Moses wandered without a home for forty years, but he had 3 million kinsmen with him. Today we usually change tents, leaving family and friends behind.

The result: loneliness. For twelve to eighteen months after a move, most people feel alone and lonely. This is especially true for a nonworking wife with children. They can't so easily get involved in a place of importance and belonging as a working husband.

When we move to a new place, we lose our place of belonging. People don't know how sociable we are! They're usually too busy with their current friends and activities to pay much special attention to us. People in our new location may think and act a lot differently than us. This often causes us to become uncertain and anxious about fitting in. Such anxiety makes it more diffi-cult for us to be the old ''lovable'' selves our old friends loved. It makes it tougher for us to initiate friendships, as well.

It takes time, persistence, and initiative to make new friends. Because of the high rate of mobility and strong desire for privacy that most Americans have, it's often hard to meet people in a new neighborhood. Your neighbors probably didn't rush over to welcome you with a freshly baked pie and a ''welcome'' when you moved in; with people coming and going so much, it didn't seem worth the effort. Besides, in most urban areas both hus-band and wife work, leaving little time for general chitchat with the neighbors. If that weren't enough, people in a neighborhood often have little in common beyond living in the same neighbor-hood. There's little natural communality to draw people together. Making friends requires repeated efforts until new acquaint-ances see us as beneficial to know and start reciprocating our

efforts. It also takes time to "sample" people so that we find
those we like. Similar interests, tastes, ways of doing things,
socioeconomic situations, family composition, and values
increase mutual attraction. The problem is that it takes time to
get to know enough about people to decide if we'd really like to
be friends. And, of course, they've got to be coming to the same
positive conclusions about us.

Most people find themselves longing for the warm, secure
friendships they've left behind. Joe or Mary can't just drop by
anymore. When something funny or sad happens, we can't call
or run over to our friends like before. Picnics, playtimes, and
helping each other are no longer possible. Phone calls and letters
help, but they're not enough to prevent longing and loneliness.
Usually those who haven't moved are busily engaged in their
daily responsibilities and have little idea of the significance that
letters and calls have in the first months after a move.

At first nobody seems to match up to old friends. Sometimes
we're afraid to get close to others because they would be
replacements, and that strikes us as being terribly disloyal.
Furthermore, we can't stand the thought of being replaced in a
dear friend's life. So we'll often find ourselves being critical of
the way our new acquaintances think or act. This helps insure
that no one will replace the special spots in our heart. It also
insures that we'll be lonely. We may refuse to accept new ways of
doing things that are customs in our new setting because we're
afraid we'll lose our identity.

Sylvia found moving to the Midwest after living in California
for twenty-two years to be a time of intense loneliness. The
conservative farm-college culture and people were alien to her.
She withdrew at first and isolated herself from those who might
have become her friends because they weren't "good enough."
At the same time she began to doubt herself and her values; no
one else seemed to see things the way she did. She avoided
others because of her new uncertainties.

Loneliness is often intensified because we want others to take
the initiative. "After all," we moan, "they've lived here and are

settled; why don't they invite us over for tea or dinner? Why should we have to make the first step?" When invitations don't come, it's easy to feel sorry for ourselves. If we stay in the trap of wanting to be courted, we'll find ourselves more socially isolated much longer than if we shake off what "ought" to be and seize the initiative.

Sometimes women will further deepen their loneliness by alienating themselves from their husbands and families. A wife may become irritable and critical of family members. She may demand that her husband spend inordinate amounts of time at home while he's spending some evenings away, trying to learn his new job. She may center on old habits and mannerisms of family members that have always bothered her, and begin criticizing them. Depression may set in and show itself in a variety of subtle ways, including loss of interest in sexual relations with her husband. At the same time the husband is likely to pull away from his wife, failing to understand her deep needs for companionship and affirmation. Usually this phase doesn't last more than several months.

Some people who frequently have to move seem to cope by developing superficial relationships. They adjust their expectations downward and are satisfied with less-intimate friendships with others. In the short run this seems to help them face moving with less stress and loneliness. In the long run it may promote loneliness in later years when there is no one to savour old and intimate companionship with (including a life-long spouse in this day of divorce).

Divorce

Loneliness is a natural by-product of divorce. Though the divorce-initiator usually has a bit better time of it, especially if the breakup was sudden and unannounced, both partners inevitably suffer feelings of guilt, regret, inadequacy, and depression. Normally it takes two to three years for them to regain emotional stability.

Divorce produces loneliness in several ways. First, there is lingering attachment to the ex-spouse. Usually the desire to reunite is ambivalent; with the normal yearning for the lost spouse is a realization that it would probably not work. Most people continue to feel drawn to their ex-mate even if they have formed a satisfactory relationship with another person after the divorce. The feeling of attachment, of need for their former spouse, seems to be there even for those who say they don't even like him or her. In many ways this pining for the lost spouse mirrors the separation anxiety of childhood. Attachment seems to persist even though trust, respect, caring, and affection may have virtually disappeared.

The desire for continued attachment normally has longing for physical intimacy mixed with it as well. Even if there was very little tenderness or physical intimacy for a considerable period of time, there is usually a longing for the intimate moments. Those moments of union offered a certain amount of comfort and hope within the marriage, and they continue to do so in the individual's imagination. In addition, getting used to no sexual intercourse can be very difficult. A high percentage of divorced men and women engage in sexual relations after divorce, even among Christians. One survey of divorced singles at a large evangelical church found that only 9 percent of the men and 27 percent of the women remained celibate. Though most had tremendous feelings of conflict between their faith and sexual experiences, loneliness and strong sex drives were the two top reasons given for propelling them into sexual activity.[12] The emptiness of not being able to physically touch and unite in love is very real.

In most cases there is a loss of at least some friends. These may have been primarily the spouse's friends. Or, they may be "couple friends" who aren't quite sure how to relate now that the couple has broken up. Furthermore, the divorceé is often seen as a sexual threat to the female friend. It's also simply difficult for a divorced single to remain in a relationship full of reminders of when there were four instead of three. He or she may feel like a useless appendage.

Many divorced people, especially women, find it difficult to make new friends. Most divorceés with children have little time or energy left for socializing by the time they work, take care of household chores, and spend at least some time with the kids. It seems particularly hard for them to establish relationships with other men because many men seem to view young divorceés in sexual terms only. Others are frightened away when they learn that children are involved. Many times the practical need for a babysitter in order to date is a very real obstacle in forming friendships.

In most divorce cases the mother is given custody of the children. This may create a special kind of loneliness for a loving father. For example, Dan has had a painful time deciding whether to take a new job that would move him several hundred miles away from his young son. The thought of not being able to have Jeb with him regularly is almost overwhelming. He knows that Jeb looks forward to the times with his daddy and will suffer deep loneliness, maybe even feelings of rejection. Sometimes mothers create barriers between the children and their father. In these cases children may pick up the idea that the father is no good and doesn't really love them or he wouldn't have left. The result is that the children may reject their father and not want to spend time with him, even though he genuinely loves them.

It's also just plain lonely coming home to an empty house or apartment. For the one keeping the former family place there are reminders of the spouse. For the other there is a place empty of memories. Usually there is a feeling that no one really understands. Parents may be cold and nonsupportive because the divorce violates their standards and tarnishes their reputation. They may feel like parental failures and in their hurt make the divorced person feel like one also. Friends may seem to miss the mark. They may console when laughter would heal or laugh when silence is needed. They may seem superficial in their comments and advice. God often seems far away, unreachable. For Christians, there are usually intense guilt feelings associated with the divorce. God may be seen as a judge — unapproachable and condemning.

Why has divorce become such a common occurrence? Why do so many feel deep loneliness even within marriage? In the next few pages I'd like to suggest several answers to these questions.

Most modern marriages are built on sand instead of bedrock. We use our hearts more than our heads when it comes to choosing a partner. Hollywood and novels have promoted *romanticism* as the foundation of marriage. Feelings rule. Too late we discover that feelings are fickle; they run hot and cold. Romanticism deceives us into feeling that we love someone if our face flushes, our heart beats faster, and our palms perspire in their presence.

> Most of the Western notions about romantic love date back to the Middle Ages.... To amuse themselves while their husbands were away, these women [of the court] became friendly with the serenading troubadors, but high-minded as they were they wrote precise rules for such liaisons. It was through these extramarital relationships that the ideal of romantic love was first born. From this illicit beginning we developed a whole tradition about extravagantly poetic amour that still persists today. As a result, we marry for love; we divorce because we no longer love; we pine for our lost love; and we ache because we are in love. The result is that many of us blindly jump into amorous interludes without considering the consequences.[13]

For many, love has become a physiological response rather than a series of caring behaviors bound by commitment. Commitment lasts as long as we feel good. Romantic love is focused on itself. Real love centers on the loved one. Romantic love fizzles at the first sign of conflict. It has no will or determination. Mature love sticks around and works things out. Romantic love is easily distracted by someone who makes us feel more pleasure because she or he is more attractive, sexier, wealthier, or wittier. Mature love recognizes that there are weeds in the grass on the other side of the fence.

It's no wonder infidelity and divorce are so rampant when our attention is constantly drawn to appearances. The sensuality of our society encourages us to choose whatever promises to give us the most pleasure. Novelty and newness are best, according to Madison Avenue. Long-term marriages are inevitably routine and boring, we're told. The notion of planned obsolescence, it seems, has spread from cars to spouses. The result is that we are encouraged to constantly look around for a better deal — for someone who is perfect in every way, somebody who is more exciting and who will tell us how wonderful we are all the time. Somebody has forgotten to tell us that no one is perfect. Such searching only brings a breakdown of trust, the dissolution of marriages, and loneliness.

Choosing a partnership that will last requires a clear head, not a pounding pulse. Unfortunately, much of today's dating focuses on the latter. It's gotten so that dating partners move from introduction to heavy petting in three dates. The results are disastrous. Approximately one out of every four brides in the U.S. are pregnant on their wedding day. Between 40 and 50 percent of couples who conceived premaritally are not together five years later. Premarital pregnancy seems to short-change the courtship process. Many of the couples are not really economically prepared for the sudden marriage which such pregnancies entail. Even among couples who don't conceive, a heavy emphasis on sex in the dating process robs them of joy. It's simply difficult to concentrate on getting to know one another when the dominant activity is sex. Cuddling cuts down communication! Most married couples spend only 5 to 10 percent of their time together in sexual activity. The rest of the time is spent wiping kids' noses, trying to stretch money to fit the month, fixing broken appliances, washing dishes, and learning to love each other in practical, nonsexual ways. This is not to discount the importance of sex. It's a delightful topping for practical love. It seals and deepens love that is built on mutual appreciation, sharing, and caring. Sexual difficulties can strain and even kill a marriage, but usually they are simply a reflection of broken understanding.

Too many dating couples have their priorities reversed. They think that good sex makes a good marriage. So they give in to their natural desires and justify sexual activity on the ground that it's helping them to know if they're compatible. In fact, a good marriage makes good sex. Emotional compatibility is the true indicator of marital success. Many couples spend 5 percent of their time developing the kind of understanding and dialogue which makes for deep, sustained intimacy, and 95 percent on physical intimacy. Our society and its insatiable emphasis on pleasure promotes this. But when it comes to lasting marriage, learning to pray together goes much further than (sexually) playing together!

Romantic love flies in the face of reality. Try to tell a teenager who is "smitten" by true love that more than twice as many men who are married before age twenty end up divorced as those who marry in their late twenties. See if he'll believe that more than twice as many women who marry before eighteen are divorced as those who wait until their early twenties. The usual response is, "That may be true, but it won't happen to us." Maybe not. But more probably it will. Intimacy is built on the commitment of two persons who are reasonably secure in who they are and where they're headed in life. A clear sense of identity precedes the ability for satisfying intimacy. Because most teens are still in the process of discovering and shaping themselves, they will change significantly. If they marry too young, they're simply gambling that their spouses will change in compatible ways. Often that doesn't happen. The result is divorce. Romantic love similarly dismisses the facts that an inadequate education and lower incomes (for men) are highly related to divorce. It rejects the contention that similarity of values is vitally important for lasting marriage. For example, studies show that couples with the same religious faith are much more likely to persevere in marriage than couples who differ or who have no religious commitment. Similarity of backgrounds and values gives a couple a head start on understanding each other. It also makes it more likely they'll be able to harmoniously establish goals and make decisions.

The best indicator of a successful marriage is not the degree of passion the couple feels but how well they know each other before marriage and how well they can communicate. Serious courting partners need to talk about life goals, lifestyles, dreams, children, husband-wife roles, and the place of their faith. It comes as little surprise to me, for example, that Christian couples who meet and date solely within the confines of a small, residential Christian college and marry shortly after graduation often end up divorcing. They've only gotten to know each other in a restricted, somewhat unrealistic environment. Couples need to get to know each other's families, and relate to each other as responsible adults in a variety of ''real-life'' settings. What is the partner like after a hard day at work? How does he relate to kids? How does he respond to sickness? If a couple has difficulty making decisions or doesn't handle conflicts well before marriage, those problems are normally worse afterward. If the two have difficulty talking with each other while dating, they'll have trouble in marriage.

Another major influence that encourages divorce is the increasing emphasis in our society on *personal rights* — individual freedom is the highest good. Freedom is to be guarded at all costs, even the loss of love. Each party (they can hardly be called partner) in the marriage stands ready to assert his own way with absolute finality. Adjustment or compromise is weakness: ''If I can't have my way, I'll leave.'' This is nothing more than sophisticated self-centeredness. Putting personal rights on the throne introduces power as the central dynamic in the relationship instead of love. Marriage becomes a glorified arm-wrestling contest. Decision-making becomes more like a tug of war. When partners are concerned primarily with themselves, they find that intimacy is impossible. To become emotionally intimate we have to be vulnerable. To be vulnerable we have to believe that our partner cares deeply about our well-being. If we can't be reasonably sure that he's on our side, we won't be able to trust. Without trust there is no intimacy.

Marriages simply can't survive if both partners don't work toward ''we-ness.'' Much of the personal rights emphasis is on ''me-ness.'' A startling example of this is illustrated in a suggested ''marriage contract'' that recently appeared in *Woman's Day* magazine:

> I will not give come-on signals to others for sexual relations when I see that you feel threatened . . . *we are separate people with our own standards and they must never be fused into one* [italics mine]. . . . I cannot make you happy or unhappy, but I can make myself happy. . . . I accept my ultimate aloneness and responsibility for myself.

Sounds like some marriage, doesn't it? Marriage without mutual attempts to give up individual rights is no marriage. Without fusion there can only be friction. Anything less is a self-seeking, rationalized escape from responsible love. The highest expression of love has always been self-sacrifice, not self-seeking. When we love, we're willing to temporarily put aside our welfare for the benefit of our loved one. The highest example of love is Jesus Christ. He gave up His personal freedom to die on our behalf. We must become like Him, a self-sacrificing individual. An overemphasis on personal rights will only set us on the defensive and make us self-protectors.

Is it any wonder that divorces have increased in this individualistic climate? Meshing the personalities, wills, and spirits of two people is tough enough even when they're committed to make it work. It becomes impossible (even unwanted) when individual rights are the rule. This orientation introduces a qualified commitment to the relationship — "I'll stay together with you as long as I feel like it." Qualified commitments simply don't last on the ups and downs of marital sailing.

Shirley Johnson, an economist from Vassar College, estimates that the chance of divorce increases by 2 percent for every additional thousand dollars a woman earns. This statistic, however, does not provide a rationale for underpaying a married woman! Equal pay ought to be given for equal work. The women's liberation movement correctly recognizes that in secular terms, money equals power. The movement has attempted to give women worth by giving them an ideal image — the working, professional woman who is able to make her own decisions because she is no longer economically dominated by a man. Certainly some women have been oppressed by their husbands. But to solve the problem by a call to power is no solution. It only insures the total breakdown of relationships. How much better it would be if women issued a call to love instead of imitating the shaky basis of economic self-worth that men have been locked into! How much better for future daughters and wives if they trained their sons to love with sensitivity and democracy! How much better for men to learn to model the compassion of women than for women to model the competitive, cutthroat behaviors of the "successful" businessman! For God's people especially, love, not power, is the key to worth.

Some marriages also disintegrate because of *neurotic patterns* that are established in the couple's relationship. One partner may dominate until the submissive partner becomes only a shell of a person. This destroys the possibility of genuine adult intimacy, which must be between equals.

The neurotic use of anger is one tool that a partner sometimes uses to establish dominance and retain control. Anger isn't always shouting and pounding; it can also be carefully barbed hostility delivered with a whisper. Usually when we get angry we don't listen very well. If this becomes a dominant response when we don't like something, it will insure both misunderstanding and alienation. We need to lead with our ears, not our mouth! Anger crushes the spirit of the partner. It makes him or her afraid to reveal real feelings for fear of an outburst. It drives partners apart into loneliness, even while it gives an element of power to one.

Of course people with even more-serious emotional dysfunctions such as depression, hysteria, and anxiety-attacks will find it difficult to establish or maintain an intimate marriage. In some respects neurosis is like the personal rights orientation, though it is certainly not as rational. Neurotic people are enmeshed in self-defensive strategies which make vulnerability virtually impossible. They find it difficult to open up and trust another for fear of rejection (both by others and themselves). Usually there is a puzzling sort of inability for people to ''get close'' to people with neurosis. This is because, emotionally, they are afraid to be known. People who doubt themselves will find it difficult to allow another person entrance into their deepest emotions and private selves because they doubt that anyone can love the ''real'' them. Those with low self-esteem and self-doubt have special problems in being able to accept or give love.

The Empty Nest

For many couples, the time when children leave home is traumatic. There's an empty room or empty chair at the table. It's a poignant reminder that time has marched on. Nothing will ever be the same. There will be no more childish laughter or talking about school triumphs and defeats. No more talk about girl friends or boy friends; no more teen pranks, pennants, or dolls in his or her room; no more ''drink your milk'' or ''clean your plate.''

If parents have focused all their attention and energies on the children for the previous twenty years, they will also face the loneliness of living with a virtual stranger. What should they talk about with each other? What can they do to fill the empty evenings or weekends? Who *is* this person they're living with?

Some marriages will fail at this point. Others will begin the new adventure of learning to know each other as persons (not just as parents). They'll find things in their partners to be delighted about. And they'll enjoy the increased freedom and finances to do things together.

Usually a mother feels the emptiness most, especially if she has not developed interests outside the home. Volunteer activities, or a part-time job when her children reach school age, help many to cope. But if a woman has not developed these outlets, she needs to actively begin pursuing them or she is likely to have problems with depression and loneliness. Sitting around in an empty house with little to do but think about the kids isn't a very positive procedure. This is especially true if the empty nest occurs in the same time span as menopause.

At the same time that parents are adjusting to their empty nest, young college freshmen choke back the homesickness that threatens to overcome them. They long in their first months away for Mom's cooking, a hug from Dad, the security of their room, and sisters and brothers. In fact, college freshmen are among the loneliest people around, according to a number of studies. It takes a while for them to adjust to really being on their own — alone, as well as to make new friends. As much as they have sought to be independent, there are still the moments of nostalgia and loneliness that come, especially under stress. As time goes on, the young adults will make new friends and normally reshape their relationship with their parents into a satisfying adult-adult friendship. But the first months are often agonizing.

Death

In other kinds of loss we can still cling to the hope of reunion. Not so with death. There is no restoration of our loved one's presence. Death's separation is final. Only memories remain, mixed with the ache of loneliness. Dan's description of his inner emptiness graphically describes the loneliness of death:

My mother died when I was 12 years old. I have always felt as
if someone needlessly took her from me and my family.
Surprisingly enough, I have always felt somewhat depressed
because of this. There always seems to be a void in my life,
because she meant so much to me — and she will never be
replaced. She was the only person who really could understand
me and be able to make me not feel lonely.

Many people, like Dan, must during their formative years endure
the deep loss of a parent. For others it is the loss of a husband or
wife, an especially close friend, a grandparent, or a brother or
sister that plunges them into grief and loneliness. Among adults,
the death of a spouse is probably life's most stressful event.
Death of close family members and friends is also among the
most stressful things that will ever happen to us.

Our first response to a loved one's death is shock. Our whole
physical and emotional system feels numb. We have difficulty
really believing that his or her life is ended. We may feel angry
and bitter toward our lost one and toward God. Usually we
experience acute grief shortly after learning of the death (in
cases of lingering illness or expected death much of the shock
and grief may actually *precede* death so that there is little
apparent distress at the time of death). We experience waves of
emotional distress and feel weak all over. These feelings are
triggered by thoughts of the lost one, as well as by expressions of
sympathy from others. Often, in our grief, we may feel distant
from other people. We become intensely preoccupied with
thoughts and images of our loved one. We may find ourselves
feeling irritated and hostile toward others, even though they're
making special efforts to comfort. We may feel as though no one
else really matters now.

During the period immediately following death we are normally surrounded by other people. It is usually in the weeks *after*
the funeral that the loneliness sets in. It may be triggered by a
certain time of day that we used to spend with our loved one.
Often the late night or early morning hours are times when

husband and wife share their love and their thoughts. The loneliness may be brought on by special days — an anniversary, Christmas, a birthday, or summer vacation times. Certain places where moments of joy, triumph, tears, or tragedy were shared may flood us with memories and emptiness. We may read a joke or hear a good piece of music on the radio and find ourselves starting to talk to our loved one, only to suddenly remember he is no longer there.

Some find the loneliness too overwhelming. They die from broken hearts. Probably all of us know of couples who have been married for many years and then die within a few months of each other. Over 70 percent of the time these deaths are officially due to coronary thrombosis or arteriosclerosis — diseases of the heart. There are many documented cases of near simultaneous deaths as well. Among cases cited by Dr. George Engel is that of a 52-year-old man who had seen his physician regularly during his wife's struggle with terminal lung cancer. A complete physical exam six months prior to her death showed no indication of heart disease, but he died suddenly of a heart attack the day after his wife's funeral.[14] Suicide rates are also higher among widowed people than they are among married people. The incidence of suicide is about two and a half times greater in the first year after a loved one's death.[15]

Death may also separate us from remaining loved ones. This is especially true in the case of parents who lose a child. There are almost always some guilt feelings when a loved one dies; this is exaggerated when a child dies. We may blame ourselves for the genetic abnormality or for not being careful enough. Parents may also try to handle their grief by blaming each other. Unless they are mature and supportive, they may end up in an endless cycle of alienating recriminations that bring hurt, isolation, and divorce. Brothers and sisters may let lust for the estate lead to unresolved conflict, bitterness toward each other, and alienation that lasts for years. Many once-close relationships have been broken by the greed of family members.

What about the loneliness of the person who is dying? About 60 percent of all deaths in America occur in impersonal, isolated hospital rooms. As people grow sicker and closer to death, fewer and fewer people visit them. In their hour of greatest need they are often alone. Many have pointed out that talking about death seems to be taboo in our society. We consequently cast dying people into a strange sort of isolation. Neither they nor us feel free to discuss feelings about the impending death. Many go to their graves unable to reveal their deepest feelings about their last days to those who matter the most to them. I'll never forget my gratitude toward my great-grandfather. I lived several hundred miles away during the last few years of his life and could visit only occasionally. Our relationship was very warm and close in spite of the miles. The last time I saw him, we talked freely about his past, his wife who preceded him in death a number of years before, his death (he felt he would die before we saw each other again), and heaven. He died several months later, but my fond memories continue because of his life and those precious hours of direct discussion of his death. Certainly there are some who don't get much past denial and anger as they face their death. They're not able to talk about it. And yet, as Elisabeth Kübler-Ross has demonstrated, the presence of a caring, trained listener can help people talk about and accept their death.[16] Instead of isolation in their last days, they are able to experience deep intimacy. Fear of death in secular America, which has led to the death taboo and physical isolation of the dying, has robbed both the dying and the grieving of perhaps the most intimate communion possible. Many die lonely.

Part 2

Relief from Loneliness

8
COPING WITH LONELINESS

By now you're probably wondering what to do about the loneliness that you, or others you care about, feel. In this last section we'll suggest ways that you can handle loneliness and build intimacy.

The first thing you need to remember is that *loneliness is normal*. We simply can't escape it. I've talked with some people who say they've never been lonely. That may be true. Often, though, we suppress our memories of loneliness because they're so painful. When I was first approached to help a student do a project on loneliness, I couldn't remember ever being lonely. My life at that point was filled with the love of family and friends. Upon further reflection, however, I began to remember different times in my life when loneliness had been my companion. But even if we have never experienced loneliness, it is likely that a move, death, divorce, or feeling of rejection will eventually face us with the experience. When it does, we need to remember that loneliness is common. This understanding will free us a bit to allow ourselves and others to express our feelings when we're hurting and empty. By accepting the experience we'll be better able to accept ourselves and others. In so doing we take a big step toward the kind of intimate communication which helps us overcome our loneliness.

Viewing most loneliness as natural, given fallen human nature and society, should help us to face our feelings. We can be more accurate in understanding ourselves and others, as well as more adequate in helping. Extreme, chronic loneliness, of course, is not normal or healthy. It signifies deep feelings of inadequacy, isolation, and insecurity. People who feel worthless and unable to make or maintain close relationships should see a professional counselor who can more systematically help them reorient their lives.

You also need to keep in mind that *loneliness has some fringe benefits*. We can learn some important things if we're willing to put up with some heartache. Loneliness gives us opportunities for self-evaluation and reorientation. It may tell us that there are things we need to change. Perhaps we're not assertive enough, or maybe we're too aggressive. Maybe we try too hard to develop friendships and drive people off. We may be too dependent on one or two others for meeting our emotional needs. Perhaps our values are too competitive or self-centered. Possibly we need to develop new interests in order to meet different kinds of people. Maybe people don't get close to us because of unresolved conflicts and bitterness that they sense within us. It could be that we're so serious about life that we're not even enjoyable to be around. Or we may be so superficial that people can't get past first base with us and give up. You get the picture, I'm sure. Use loneliness for evaluation and reorientation, as a launching pad for new patterns of life. Don't wallow in self-analysis.

Another fringe benefit of loneliness is that it provides us with a chance to learn *positive solitude*. When we're lonely *and* alone, we can either be overwhelmed by emptiness or we can positively use our aloneness. Positive solitude allows us to face ourselves when we're by ourselves. It's using the time and silence to get in touch with ourselves, with God, and with our future. Instead of running from our loneliness by turning on a record player, radio, or television, we allow ourselves to hear our thoughts and experience our feelings. The silence and our loneliness may encourage us to turn our thoughts to God as well. We may be better able to hear His "still, small voice" which is often submerged in a whirlwind of people and activity. As He speaks to us in our lonely solitude, He often allows us special experiences of intimacy with Him that leave us feeling loved and cared for.

Loneliness can also stir us to appreciate our friendships. We can easily take for granted those who matter most to us. We may get so locked into the routines of living that we fail to take time to enjoy and affirm our spouse, children, and close friends. The loneliness of temporary separation, or the more tragic loneliness of loss, may shock us into reassessing our priorities and putting more into our closest relations.

As we recognize the fringe benefits of loneliness, some of our fears will subside. Sad is not always bad, though it may *feel* that way. Realizing that we can't completely escape loneliness takes some of the pressure off as well. Sometimes it seems that people are so afraid of loneliness that they get involved in relationships and behavior patterns much more damaging than the actual loneliness.

Effective and Ineffective Coping

Even though we realize that loneliness is somewhat normal and there are some fringe benefits, most of us still want to get rid of it. What are the best ways to cope with loneliness? What kind of responses are ineffective? Before we get into specific coping strategies, I'd like to report what my colleague, Ray Paloutzian, and I have found.

As you might expect, friends are vitally important. About 68 percent of the several hundred people we surveyed felt that talking to a close friend about their feelings was moderately to highly effective. Almost 58 percent said that simply spending time with a friend, just to be together, was effective.

Other behaviors that our respondents found moderately to highly helpful were getting alone to think (56.7 percent), listening to music (48.5 percent), prayer (42 percent), and reading (36.4 percent). It is likely that these behaviors are more effective for some kinds of loneliness than others. Listening to music and reading, for example, are probably most effective with loneliness due to the temporary absence of a friend or family members. They're also likely to be only temporarily effective. Loneliness remedies that last involve more active planning.

Some behaviors are clearly ineffective. Overeating is something a lot of people do when they're lonely. Only about 12 percent of the people we interviewed found eating to be effective. Some people try to substitute physical intimacy for emotional intimacy when they're lonely. They feel that sexual relations with someone will bring them close to another and meet their deep inner need for communion. Fewer than 10 percent of the people we talked with found sex to be the answer. Others try to forget their loneliness by escaping through alcohol or drugs. Each of these responses numbs reality. Neither helps the person face his or her loneliness effectively. About 6 percent of our interviewees found them moderately effective. We also learned that people who have better social skills are the most likely to see these and other diversionary behaviors as ineffective.

Another behavior that will plunge us into despair is feeling sorry for ourselves. When we feel sorry for ourselves, we're really saying that we're *not* at fault for our loneliness and that nothing can be done about it. Feeling sorry goes hand in hand with blaming — ''*If only* Fred hadn't done that, or Joyce hadn't done that.'' Feeling sorry is another way of saying, ''Why me? I deserve better.'' Because it denies any personal responsibility, there can be no effective strategy for conquering loneliness while we let self-pity have the floor.

Feeling sorry for ourselves usually is associated with withdrawal. It's a way of protecting our fractured ego. Unfortunately, it only assures a deepening of our loneliness. Withdrawal encourages us to think about ourselves, about how things might have been, and to become immersed in our feelings. Usually we need others to give us perspective and lift us out of the emotional quicksand we find ourselves in when we're lonely.

Helping Yourself

Ultimately, *we are responsible* for our own loneliness. We are the ones who feel it, and we're the ones who have to do something about it. If we sit back passively and wait for a relationship to be restored or a new one to be formed, it won't happen. If we blame our lonely situation on someone else, we'll only feel bitter. If we blame it on ourselves, we'll only feel defeated. The first step in overcoming loneliness is to face it and accept the responsibility for coping with it.

Among other things this means to *think positively*. Granted, that may be tough to do when we're down. Thinking positively does not mean putting on an artificial smile. What I'm talking about is an orientation. Chronically lonely people are typically pessimistic; they blame themselves. They're likely to think that they're lonely because they're worthless, ugly, stupid, insensitive, or dull. Hand in hand with self-blame go depression and hopelessness. In addition, lonely people make negative social predictions. They get stuck in their loneliness because they see no future in various relationships. They feel as though it's no use continuing a relationship or starting a new one. They think that they'll *never* meet anyone they'll really be happy with, or that those they're attracted to won't like them. They feel as though there's no place to meet people with similar values and interests. They expect to be lonely because of their pessimism.

One way to decrease loneliness, then, is to increase our positive thoughts and decrease our negative ones. There are several approaches that we can take.[1] One is to interrupt our negative thought when we notice we're producing one, and go back to a positive thought. If we need a stronger interruption, and can be alone, we can actually think a negative thought — then yell "STOP!" at ourselves as loudly as we can. Then we can think positive thoughts and tell ourselves, "Good." We should practice until we can silently scream STOP! and can use it in public. Another approach is to snap ourselves smartly on the wrist with a rubber band when we think negatively. To help increase our positive thoughts we should write down anything positive we can think of about ourselves on index cards. Then when we periodically look at the cards we'll be thinking positive thoughts. Pair positive thoughts with daily behavior routines — putting shoes on, driving to work, and so forth. We should also take notice of the things we accomplish each day and give ourselves a pat on the back. It's interesting isn't it, that Paul commands Christians: "Whatever is true, whatever is noble, whatever is right, whatever is pure, whatever is lovely, whatever is admirable — *if anything is excellent or praiseworthy — think about such things!*" (Philippians 4:8, italics added). Positive thinking is not a gimmick — it's an essential for preventing and overcoming loneliness.

Another way to handle pessimism is to write down any negative thought we may have and indicate how our thought makes us feel and behave. Then either by ourselves or with a close friend we should examine past relationships to see if they support or counter our thought. Check your thought (for example, "Girls won't go out with me because they think I'm boring") with some friends to see if it's accurate. Then write down a convincing, rational counterthought (for example, "Girls have gone out with me and had a good time"). Whenever possible we should try to *externalize* the cause of our loneliness. If we can see our loneliness as due to some external and temporary situation, we're well on our way to overcoming pessimism and hopelessness. People who can do this are more likely to expect social success in the future. Try not to blame other people, though, or you may end up feeling hostile. Give them the benefit of the doubt. Try to see their actions as due to circumstances rather than personality traits or malicious intentions.

Building self-esteem is crucial for us to be optimistic. If we are down on ourselves the whole world will look like a continuous summer storm. Negative thoughts are usually planted by people who are important to us. Parents, teachers, close friends, or a respected colleague may make comments that tell us we don't meet their expectations. Their disappointment may be expressed in cutting remarks or more-subtle put-downs. This negative feedback normally knocks us out of kilter. The more that we have felt devalued and criticized, the more difficult it will be for us to change our self-esteem. But, we *can* change sufficiently to give us a positive outlook on ourselves and our lives.

One way to begin is to imagine *in detail* the kind of person we'd like to be. We should picture ourselves doing things the way we'd like to but don't think we can now. We should imagine ourselves receiving praise and gratitude from others for who we are and things we do. We need to feel ourselves accepting the affirmation. We must think about things we need to do to become the way we want to be, and see ourselves doing those things. We must hear the people who may have put us down saying very specific positive things which contradict their earlier responses.

We must admit our weaknesses and acknowledge that we're sinners. But we should not accept the notion that there's nothing good about us. In comparison with God's complete perfection we are nothing; but compared with others we each have characteristics we can affirm. Avoid "I'll never" (be able to do this) or "Nobody will ever" (like me) thoughts. Reward yourself for specific things you've done well each day by telling yourself, "I sure did...well."

Remember that God loves you and accepts you as you are. As one little boy said, "God made me, and He don't make junk!" God knows that we'll make mistakes. He also knows that we're self-centered and sinful. Sometimes we get down on ourselves because we fail to meet our own spiritual or moral standards. God grants us forgiveness upon confession and repentance. Furthermore, He forgets our sin when He forgives, and He doesn't continually remind us how bad we are. Satan does that.

Rather, God tells us how much He loves us, and how He delights in us when our hearts are set on following Him. The fact that God loves us gives us a firm foundation for loving ourselves. After all, He doesn't make mistakes! As we become immersed in His Word, fellowship with Him in confession, and experience His working in our lives, we become more and more certain of our own worth.

Optimism is greatly increased as we are able to believe God is in control, that *He* has not abandoned us. If we really trust in God's continuous, personal care, we will find it difficult to be pessimistic. To the extent that we believe in practical ways that "In all things God works for the good of those who love him . . ." (Romans 8:28*a*), we will find hope and strength. We will find it difficult to think pessimistically about our future or to be in total despair about our present. It's difficult to start believing this way in the middle of a deep crisis. The time to begin believing is before, in the day-to-day, "normal" ups and downs. As we trust God in this way we'll find our burdens lifted. This *doesn't* mean that we should stop planning for the future and just passively trust God. But it does mean we will begin to see events that are out of our control as under His control. We must begin to trust outcomes to His care. We must also become increasingly able to see the things that are "bad" as opportunities for God to shape our character, to lead in new directions that are ultimately better for us. I've heard more than one person eventually thank God for breakups of engagements, for example, because they knew it never would have worked, and God had a better way for them. In one sense, optimism is faith. It is faith that God is there, caring, and working in difficult circumstances to bring about the best for us. As we learn to trust God's intentions and competency, we discover that there is good reason for optimism. Too often we give up on God before He's finished molding us.

We mentioned earlier that feeling helplessness, loneliness, and depression go together. One form of helplessness is self-pity. As long as we allow ourselves to wallow in self-pity, we'll

remain trapped in loneliness. When we've lost a close relationship, a certain period of grieving and loneliness is both healthy
and probably unavoidable. We can't deny our feelings! If we do,
we're liable to respond with an emotional backswing and jump
into relationships we'll later regret. After a while, though, we'll
become aware that it's time to pick up the pieces and move
ahead. At that point we need to adopt a problem-solving orientation and develop a plan. I believe that self-pity is one of the
greatest obstructions to overcoming loneliness.

The first thing we need to do is *identify the primary cause of
our loneliness*. Sometimes this is fairly easy. We may be quite
aware that we started feeling lonely after our close friend moved
to another state. Sometimes identifying the cause may be more
difficult. We feel that we're far from God and feel as though our
prayers don't get any higher than our ceiling. It would be easy to
attribute our loneliness to a lack of fellowship with God. And
that may indeed be the case. On the other hand, we may feel
distant from God because of an unresolved conflict with someone
that has bred bitterness. In that case we'll find our loneliness
disappearing, and our relationship with God reappearing, when
we genuinely forgive and restore our relationship with our
"enemy."

The reason we need to identify the primary cause of our
loneliness is that this will help us to decide on a specific plan of
action. If we only know that we're feeling lonely, we may try
ineffective ways of coping. In table 8.1 I have listed several
causes of loneliness — most of them have already been discussed.

Once we have determined the main reason *why* we're lonely,
we should *develop a plan of action* for overcoming it. We must
establish specific goals that we believe will result in the removal
of loneliness (e.g., making two new friends in the next six
months). We have to be realistic, however, and realize that we
cannot expect to change our entire personality in one week.
Instead, we should decide on several specific actions we can do
at specific times during the next days or weeks that will help us
overcome our loneliness. As we move through this section on

relief, we'll touch on some specific ways to help overcome loneliness for a number of these root causes. When we do those things, don't forget the verbal pat on the back. Keeping a chart that we can check off is also rewarding.

Our plan of action depends upon us for success. If we must depend on someone else's initiative or responses, we may never accomplish our goal. There are several elements of a good plan.[2] First, it must involve small or manageable steps. Second, it should be specific so that we can imagine ourselves doing it. Third, it should seem reasonable or workable, not something we know we won't be able to accomplish. Fourth, our plan must be a positive one. We should never plan negatively ("I'm not going to stay in my room this weekend"), but state it affirmatively ("I'm going to go to a concert this weekend. I'm going to invite a friend to go with me").

Table 8.1

PRIMARY ROOTS OF LONELINESS

Lack of confidence in yourself (low self-esteem)
Shyness
No one to play with (children)
Unresolved conflict with someone
Physical separation from loved ones
Sin
Rejected by parents (specify reason)
Rejected by friends (specify reason)
Rejected by work partners (specify reason)
Criticism by people you look to for affirmation
Death of parent
Death of brother or sister
Death of your child
Death of a close friend or relative
Breakup of a dating or courting relationship

Divorce
Feeling misunderstood
Just moved to a new place
A close friend just moved
Children leave home
Desiring a relationship that isn't happening
Not spending fellowship time with God
Illness
Not taking initiative to make friends
Not knowing how to make friends
Feeling unneeded
Retirement
Too busy studying or working to spend time with friends
Being alone in a strange place
Feeling you don't belong
Visiting or immigrating to another country
Separation from family and loved ones during holidays

Another thing we may have to do is adjust our expectations. Often people are lonely because of a mismatch between their desired and achieved levels of intimacy. Often our plans are too lofty, and we must reduce our desires and expectations. It may be that we need to reduce the amount of contact we desire. This will certainly not be easy, but in the long run it will lessen our pain. For example, it's unrealistic to expect our spouses to listen avidly to everything we want to say every night. It's a good idea. though, to set aside some time each week for special "deep" conversation instead. We probably won't experience the level of companionship that we're used to and desire if our wife or husband of forty years dies. But that doesn't mean we will have to do without companionship. Rather, it means we'll have to reduce our desires. It appears that over time lonely people automatically do some of this adapting. A trap that some people fall into is to idolize and idealize certain relationships. Single people may make marriage into a fantasy that is even beyond heaven. They may feel that *if only* they could get married they'd have all their emotional needs met. Some married people look at the grass on the other side of their marital fence and think that the other person and they would make a great pair, much better than the current link-up. Even people who have lost a loved spouse may make their departed husband or wife into such a saint that no one could possibly match up to them. In so doing they cut themselves off from the possibility of a new, different, but also satisfying remarriage. If you idolize and idealize, you'll find yourself never satisfied with the way things are. Fantasy is just that — always better than reality. But we have to live in reality. How much better to focus our appreciation on the way things are.

Another way to reduce the desired-achieved gap is by finding ways to increase our social contacts. We may do this by meeting new friends or by more fully using our existing network of friends. We may start spending more time with people and less time on other activities. By locating groups that do things we like to do, we can meet new friends. Our interests and hobbies can be used as a social door handle. How can we find such groups or events? A local community newspaper is ideal for locating people or groups whose interests are similar to ours. The telephone book is also helpful. Often you can find specific kinds of organizations listed there. Many larger cities have resource books of community organizations that may also provide help. Finally, we may just need to start paying closer attention to the people already around us at work, in our neighborhood, or in our churches. Often we overlook people who have compatible interests and personalities because we don't reach out enough to find out about them.

Remember that ''loneliness is not forever.''[2] When we're depressed and lonely it seems as though time drags. It may also seem that no one will ever fill the emptiness, and our pain will continue forever. It won't. If we take active steps and work at it, things will change. This doesn't mean we'll cavalierly continue on our way with no painful memories. But we'll find the immense and immediate pain will begin to lessen. Even if we do nothing, the hurt will eventually subside. We're built so that we can only handle so much stress. After a while we begin to habituate to hurt as a means of emotional survival. In a sense that's what is meant by "time heals." We must continually reassure ourselves that our loneliness won't last forever, that God and other people will fill the void if we let them.

We shouldn't be seduced into hostility or individualism as a means of handling our hurt. A recent book purports to teach people how to quickly fall out of love.[3] The author claims a success rate of 100 percent over five years. Among the techniques she uses are silent ridicule and repulsion of the former partner. Repulsion includes picturing the former mate covered with excrement. It's certainly likely that hate will end a relationship. But it will also scar the heart for future relationships. It certainly isn't God's way to handle loneliness! Individualism will try to convince us that the way to go is to protect our rights and demand our way. That way we won't be the victim in future relationships. Whether we initiate a breakup or not doesn't change the truth — we and our partner are both victims when individualism reigns, because we are interdependent creatures.

Many people find that pets help fill the gap when they're lonely. Though pets can never completely substitute for human intimacy, they do help. One study found that people with heart disease who live alone and have pets lived longer than those with no pets. Pets give us someone to talk to, endlessly if need be. They never argue. They're almost always affirming. At times they seem to be almost human, sensing when we're sad or happy. Deep bonds are formed between people and pets that help sustain when other bonds seem to be disintegrating.

Helping Others

When we're lonely we're likely to be very self-preoccupied. It may be difficult to think of anything but our pain and the people we're cut off from. We need periods of self-examination and ventilation of our feelings through crying and talking. Eventually, though, self-focus becomes suffocating. We need to move on. One of the best ways to do that is to make other people our focus. We simply find it difficult to focus in more than one direction at a time.

In *The Devil's Advocate*, dying Monsignor Meredith reminds us that "It is no new thing to be lonely. It comes to all of us sooner or later. . . . If we try to retreat from it, we end in a darker hell. . . . But if we face it, if we remember that there are a million others like us, if we try to reach out to comfort them and not ourselves, we find in the end we are lonely no longer."[4]

Helping others in need not only shifts our focus but often results in development of new bonds. When we care for another person we find ourselves drawn to them, and they to us. We begin thinking about how to help them out of their difficulties. In the process our own problems seem smaller. We only have so much emotional energy to spend. When we spend it helping others, there's not as much left over to splurge on ourselves. For the lonely, helping others can be a valuable form of therapy.

How can we help others cope with loneliness? The truth of the matter is that there are no magic solutions. Helping someone who is lonely usually requires some degree of commitment. It takes time, energy, and patience. A few well-intentioned words like, "I know it must be hard, but you've just got to shake it off and start living again," don't suffice. Such advice will do little good. It is also likely to erect a barrier between us and the person we're trying to help. They'll think that we really don't understand if we give superficial advice in a detached, arms-length manner.

The first thing we need in order to be an effective helper is to *be aware*. It's easy to think that people are getting along fine, because they wear a socially acceptable mask which prevents them from really being seen. A former student of mine expressed this powerfully in the following poem:

ME

Inside, a void; dark, lonely, filled with emptiness
Outside a wide canyon smile; safe, tho' fake, as

The world walks by, hands in its pockets — "How are you?"

A vacuum, searching for bits, pieces, anything
Tugging, pulling at plastic smiles, plastic hearts
Which let nothing slip, nothing go, can let nothing...
"Read Matthew six."

This world of eyeless faces
Living to love, laugh, learn, but letting
My tears flow unnoticed down lonely cheeks.
"Praise the Lord, bro'!"

Bright jokes like Frisbees float gaily over the lawn.
Bright words they are, yet innocent guards over shallow
       hearts
That all love their neighbors while they look right thru
       me.

If they'd wake up, if they'd stand up, if they'd only see
My eyes screaming, "Help me, I'm lonely, I wanna be
Loved, if you'll just listen, I..."

But they turn and stroll away, well-meaning eyes
Shining as they see a friend, hear a joke
Their well-built worlds filled with fullness, no extra room.
"We love you, bro'."

                                                —P. D. Clayton

    Because of social taboos against directly expressing our deep
needs, we need to be alert to other cues. If a person has just
moved, lost a friend or loved one due to death, been divorced,
immigrated into the U.S., seems very shy, is ill, or has recently
retired, you can be reasonably sure he's having struggles. Now
don't *assume* it and go barging in with, "I know you must be
lonely so I came to cheer you up!" Rather, these cues should
sensitize us. The person may make a brief comment about
"How different it is living in this new place," or "How much I

enjoyed your last visit," or "How hard it is to meet people," or "How I miss Walter." At that point we're being given an indirect invitation to respond to his needs.

We must *make ample time* to visit them, or better yet, invite them over to our home. Give them an opening after you've talked a while about more superficial, "priming," matters with a comment like, "You've only been here two months, haven't you? I've heard that the first year after people move is often difficult. How have things been going for you?" In your comment show understanding of the life event that may be promoting their needs, but allow them the freedom to either pick up on that understanding or say no to deeper discussion.

If they want to discuss their loneliness, we must show that we *accept them*. Many people see lonely people as self-centered, complainers, and somehow to blame for their problem. If we have that kind of attitude we'll probably not be willing to take time with them in the first place. If we do take time, we'll end up making judgmental statements that try to place blame on the other person. We need to realize that *at this point in time*, the person we're listening to probably *is* self-focused, depressed, and not too pleasant to relate to. They won't always give us the social rewards of laughter, light discussion, and affirmation. But we have to stick with them and be willing to actively listen and empathize so that they will feel we're on their side when we start to more actively make suggestions. By affirming them we can help them to feel that they're not "weird" or boring because they're talking a lot. One way we can insure this is by following up any time that's been "heavy" with another invitation to get together. That simple act tells them they haven't been rejected. Mix times of sharing with times of plain enjoyment; do things together such as shopping, playing tennis, or working on a car.

Consider adopting single, widowed, or childless persons as honorary grandparents, aunts, or uncles. This has dual benefits. If your extended family lives at some distance, they can provide a special kind of emotional support for you and your kids. At the same time you help them to feel included. Make them a regular part of the family. Periodically invite them over for meals, let them babysit if they like to, and invite them on family outings. Older people with children and grandchildren at some distance, and middle-aged singles, especially seem to appreciate being needed and having a place to belong.

Obviously, we can't assist every person who seems to be lonely, but we can still communicate caring by periodic phone calls and get-togethers. Try to anticipate times when people are most likely to feel lonely — holidays, anniversaries, Sunday afternoon dinners, birthdays — so you can reach out. Small acts such as birthday cards, a "thinking of you" card, flowers on special days, on unexpected days telling them we care, and helping them to feel wanted can make a big difference.

When people have recently experienced a loss of relationship, empathy and caring can often best be expressed through touch. The power of touch to comfort stems from an apparently inbuilt need that we have for physical contact. One of the somewhat surprising things we've found in our research is the number of people who said that the *one* thing another person could do that would best help them cope with their loneliness was to hug them, hold their hand, or give them a shoulder to cry on. These responses were most often from women.

In middle-class Christian circles we have tended to outlaw touch (especially across sexes) in our attempts to control sexual impulses and meanings. It's no secret that touch can be subtly used to communicate sexual feelings. As such it is wrong (unless between marital partners). But touch can also express simple caring and bring comfort to those who are alone. Heterosexual touch must be done with pure intentions, at a time of need, in proper context, and is probably best confined to occasions when another person (husband, wife, or friend) is present. But it is appropriate. Touch between two women is generally accepted in our society; hopefully, the raucous emergence of homosexuality will not restrict the expression of comforting and affectionate nonsexual touch between women in years ahead. Touch between men as a means of expressing love and comfort has a tougher time. First, it has been regarded as nonmasculine by a society which expects the ideal man to be in perfect control and virtually emotionless. Second, the rise of gay rights and increased gay visibility makes it even more difficult for physical touch to occur without sexual connotations. Nevertheless, within the church body, we should not be afraid of it. As fathers, we should not shrink from showing affection to our sons through touch. If we teach them that it's okay, even manly, and doesn't carry sexual overtones, the men of tomorrow will be more free and able to comfort those in need.

It's vital that we *provide an opportunity for the lonely person to ventilate his feelings*, to talk about the one he's yearning for, to dream about how things were or might have been. We can help him clarify just what has caused his loneliness and what his feelings are. Usually the value of this kind of expression is lost after the first few times. Gently, but firmly, we can begin to help him start planning for the future. Don't let him dwell on his loneliness if he begins to recycle his feelings in a nonconstructive, self-pitying way. If we continue to listen we are rewarding his complaining, depression, and passivity. This doesn't mean that we should cut off brief expressions of loneliness — they can be very therapeutic.

Don't suggest too many things at once. Let the lonely person proceed one step at a time. If he has difficulty, we must be willing to give ourselves to him for definite activities. We should help him select activities that will help him reconnect with others. Go to a community event or two, a concert, an art show, or church together a few times until he gains the emotional strength he needs to initiate activities and contacts on his own. Gently but clearly we should encourage him to take initiative so that an unhealthy dependency doesn't develop. At the same time, we have to remember that one or two visits or activities a month won't help much. We have to be regularly available. If our initial contact was positively received, we should try to make phone or personal contact at least two or three times a week for a few weeks, until he is on his feet again. Passive activities like watching television don't do much to build the relationship or his emotional strength. Instead, try to do things which involve direct interaction between people.

Finally, we must *encourage* our friend to *seek the comfort of God's Spirit* by praying together and thanking God for His continuing but unfinished work in our lives. Ask Him together for the comforting and lifting work of the Holy Spirit. Seek promises in the Word that show God's love and care when others were in need. Memorize those promises together. By studying the Scriptures we can discover insights into each of our daily situations. Such insights will help a friend look beyond his loneliness to God's solutions. The Psalms are a gold mine of verses that speak to depression, loneliness, and God's faithful responses. They provide an excellent source of prayer and study.

We've seen in this chapter that our general attitude is a crucial part of dealing with our loneliness. If we cultivate a determination to focus on positive plans, avoid self-pity, take the initiative, concentrate on giving ourselves to others in need, and seek the Lord's comfort, we will find relief from loneliness. At the same time, it's important to remember that the complete removal of loneliness may be difficult or impossible for many singles who long to be married, and for those who have lost close loved ones.

9

BUILDING INTIMACY

We live in an age of impatience. We've learned to look for instant success, instant resolutions, instant replay, and instant friends. Intimacy, however, is not instant. It is not something you work to get and then can hold on to like a brick of gold. It must be developed and maintained by a continued willingness to discuss things that matter, to care for each other's needs, and to affirm each other. Otherwise it can be lost, and two people who were very close can become strangers. Friendships take time to develop; they can't be pigeonholed into definite time slots. They aren't efficient and frequently aren't convenient. Men especially are tempted to put all their time and energy into work achievements. They can become "workaholics" who view people only as stepping stones. I've heard more than one person at the end of his career express regrets that he didn't spend more time with his family and friends. Close relationships bring satisfaction that money, status, and achievements can't touch.

Intimacy also requires interdependence. Many psychology books describe mature development as movement from dependence to independence. This reflects the pervasive value of autonomy in our society. Mature development must move beyond independence to interdependence. Interdependence is the ability to give and receive love, to be willing to modify our own impulses and desires for the well-being of another, to look beyond ourselves. It involves a mutual dependence that recognizes our inability to meet our deepest needs on our own.

Because of the time, effort, and risks necessary to build intimacy, we are unlikely to have more than a few truly intimate friends — probably only one or two we can be very open with. One of the things that psychologists have found, though, is that loneliness is associated with the *satisfaction* we feel in our relationships, not the number of relationships we have. Popularity has little to do with intimacy. If you have a spouse, family member, or friend with whom you can mutually be open, it's unlikely that you'll be lonely. The one exception is that many people feel a special need for emotional intimacy with a member of the opposite sex. The apostle Paul recognized this was a strong need for many but not all (1 Cor. 7:7). For these people, close relationships with family or friends of the same sex will probably not be adequate.

Starting Friendships

How do intimate relationships begin? Most of us have seldom stopped to think about it. We haven't had to. We've enjoyed intimate friendships and feel that they just develop naturally. Unfortunately, that's not true for all of us. Even those who never before had to think about making friends often find themselves socially anxious and insecure when they move to a new city or change jobs. Some who have always had friends find they have difficulty making new friends in a new setting. Others of us have had life-long difficulty making friends. We describe ourselves as shy. We may find it difficult or impossible to talk spontaneously, we blush easily around others, and we prefer being by ourselves to avoid the stress of other people's attention toward us. Shy people are usually self-conscious and put themselves down a lot. They're highly anxious about other people's evaluations and believe that they have nothing worthwhile to contribute.

One of the first steps in developing friendships is to *be friendly* — take the initiative, start conversations, help someone in need. Shy people find it difficult to take the initiative. It's not that they're unfriendly — it's just tough for them to reach out, because they fear being rejected. If we're shy, how can we begin to reach out and develop intimacy?[1] The first thing for us to do is to draw up a contract with ourselves. If we have trouble meeting others, we must set a goal. We might want to start out simply by saying hello to five people we pass on the street this week. Our long-range ("I want to make some new friends") and short-range goals for each week should be written out. We need to keep track of our success. Our short-range goals must be realistic. Making an intimate friend in one week, for example, is unrealistic. The goals must also be built on one another. For example, we might have a goal one week of saying hello to two people at work or in our neighborhood. The next week we might set the goal of talking to them for about two minutes. The following week we might invite them to join us for a coffee break.

How can we meet people who might be good friendship possibilities, after we've had some preliminary conversations with them? Usually, friendships are built on similar interests and hobbies, common values and attitudes, similar backgrounds, and personality characteristics we find appealing. Sometimes friendships develop because an acquaintance steps forward at a time of need and really shows the kind of caring that creates a special bond; others whom we might have thought of as "better material" might not reach out in a similar way. We might also try jotting down the names of two or three casual acquaintances we'd like to get to know better. Then we might write down all we know about each of them and also list the things we have in common. Then we should take the initiative by making a phone call to check something out, get some advice, or express a thought. Invite them over for lunch or to some event. We should express our enjoyment of our time together (if we enjoyed it).

Then make plans for another get-together, although at times it's good to make spontaneous invitations. Spontaneity helps bring an element of informality and friendship into the picture much faster. People don't feel as much on the spot. It communicates the fact that we feel comfortable with them.

My wife and I have found that some of our deepest friendships have originated through joint participation in activities that express some of our deepest values: They have come out of times of discussion in small-group or one-to-one prayer times, in small Bible study groups, or through participation in musical groups. As a result of sharing fundamental concerns, we've experienced the joy of getting to know some people who have become very dear to us.

But what can we say? Most conversations begin with a greeting ("Hi! How are you?") and introduction ("My name is ..."). Usually the first meeting is fairly short and spent identifying one another — where we live, what we do, or where we come from. We should also be prepared to talk about what's happening in the news, a book, or some interesting things that have happened to us recently. Practice talking with a stranger in a grocery store or bus line. Also, try practicing an imaginary conversation in front of a mirror (full-length, if possible). Visualize the interaction — imagine what the other person will say. Our part of the talking should be done out loud. We must imagine that our mirror-image is the other person and then select a comfortable distance from that image. Our imaginary conversation should be practiced for a week before interacting with the person we'd like to meet. We can imagine being asked various questions, trying different twists on the conversation, and feeling ourselves relaxed as we handle each new twist. We should also reward ourselves as we talk by complimenting ourselves on how relaxed we are. This imaginary conversation can be used for each step of our new relationship — imagining what we'll say and what they'll say at a second meeting, and so forth. I should mention, however, that we must put all of these steps into

actual use in real-life situations or they will become no more
than useless fantasy.

One of the best ways to keep a conversation going and take the
spotlight off ourselves is to ask questions and get the other
person talking about himself. Ask questions about his background, his work, and his hobbies. Avoid questions with one
word answers: "Did you like the speaker at Garden Club last
week?" Instead, ask open-ended questions that call for *extended
answers* ("What things did you enjoy most on your vacation?"),
opinions, or *thoughts* ("How do you think . . . ?"). We can also
interject bits of information about ourselves in relation to those
questions.

Active listening is also an essential for a good conversationalist.
Most people are so involved with what they're going to say that
they really don't listen. We can affirm our partner as he talks by
nodding our head or making comments which show our interest.
We should occasionally relate his experience to a similar one
that we've had, to show that we understand (we should try not to
do it in a way that shifts the focus to ourselves though). We'll
find, if we really listen, that comments and further questions
will naturally suggest themselves to us. One warning: If we
simply ask a string of questions, our partner will begin to feel
we're a lawyer for the prosecution. By interjecting feelings of
our own, we give the other person a chance to ask some questions
of us.

Sometimes we find that others seem to avoid us, or seem to
back off after they've talked with us a few times. If this happens
often, we need to evaluate ourselves. It's likely that we're doing
some things that make others uncomfortable. If we have a close
friend we can talk with candidly, we should ask him if he's
noticed any things about us that might turn people off. Some
possibilities are: unpleasant facial expression, poor grooming,
not making eye contact, complaining or talking too much about
our problems, not showing interest in what others are saying,
criticizing others, speaking too softly, pausing too long when

it's our turn to respond, cutting others off or finishing sentences for them, demanding to be with others too often or when it's not convenient, not laughing or joking, not joining in conversations when others are present, or not initiating conversation, including the expression of our thoughts and feelings. Any of these habits may make relating to us costly or unenjoyable.

Before we examine more closely the process of becoming intimate, it's important to mention that most of us need more than one intimate friendship. Usually we find that we are intimate in different ways and on different levels with various people. Though a spouse may (and should) know us more deeply than others, we need others as well. We find we can talk with a friend about things our wife or husband might not understand. This is healthy as long as confidences are kept. It takes some of the stress off one person trying to bear all of our concerns and respond with total understanding, which is humanly impossible.

For a relationship to deepen there must be a sense of enjoyment and trust between two people. Enjoyment usually stems from shared interests and things about another person's personality that complement us. We find pleasure in people who seem to look at life as we do. Similarity affirms who we are and the choices we make. It provides us with a sense of security. Similarity also provides a better foundation of understanding. Those from similar backgrounds or similar experiences are more likely to be sensitive and understanding of our needs. They can anticipate and empathize because they've been there. The apostle Paul was able to endure even suffering because he saw it, and his experience of God's comfort, as a way of touching lives: "Praise be to the God and Father of our Lord Jesus Christ, the Father of compassion and the God of all comfort, who comforts us in all our troubles so that we can comfort those in any trouble with the comfort we ourselves have received from God" (2 Corinthians 1:3-4). It's not that those with different orientations are "insensitive" (a pejorative term), but they will normally find it more difficult to pick up on need cues or to know how to respond. We're simply more compatible.

We'll return to the notion of compatibility a bit later when we talk about marriage. At the same time we look for those who are similar, we also enjoy poeple who complement aspects of our personality. If we tend to be very serious we may like people who are more lighthearted and zestful. If we're unable to organize even our weekly grocery list, we may admire and enjoy someone who has the gift of administration. If we're very quiet and shy, we may be attracted to people who are more extroverted. To a certain extent opposites do attract. But our differences must be bonded with the glue of basic similarities. Too much difference means tension and dissension. Too much similarity leads to boredom. A blending of the two provides security and scintillation in our relationship.

Going Deeper

Moving into deeper levels of intimacy may be seen as a process of social penetration.[2] Social penetration requires growing trust and disclosure between two people — no risk, no intimacy. Our personality can be thought of as an onion. There are layers of things to be known about each of us. On the outside are our acts, ideas, and beliefs — things which are fairly accessible to the people around us. These include biographical facts, opinions about noncontroversial issues, and interests and hobbies we don't consider too personal. As we move inward the number of items decreases. They represent our deep-seated values, self-attitudes, fears, and dreams. The deeper we go, the more we deal with feelings and beliefs that involve the total personality. These core characteristics are generally very private. To reveal them is to become vulnerable to hurt, because they often contain real or perceived weaknesses which we hold about ourselves, things which could be exploited.

The process of social penetration involves a gradual deepening and broadening of our self-disclosure to another person. As we gradually reveal more, we watch carefully to see how our partner responds. Does he keep confidences, or does he talk to others about us? Does he laugh at our disclosures? Does he seem to grasp how vulnerable we're making ourselves? Does he seem to disclose things about himself of a similar nature? Does he seem to understand what our needs are?

We become willing to risk more and more of ourselves as we determine that our partner is trustworthy. We must be convinced that our friend is interested in promoting our welfare. As we experience times of enjoyment together and develop attraction, we become willing to test out his trustworthiness. Usually this involves taking a small risk with some information or possessions. If he responds with apparent care, we then become willing to risk a bit more. At each point we're sensitive to signs of affirmation or rejection. Untrustworthiness, which is felt as rejection, may be communicated in a variety of ways: failure to keep a promise, divulging secrets, failure to respond appropriately, critical responses to our disclosures, inconsistency in the relationship, and unreliability when we ask him for a favor.

Seeing our partner as trustworthy is not just dependent on his actions, however. Our own personality and previous experiences greatly affect our ability to see others as trustworthy and to trust them. We filter the responses of others through the framework of our personality and past. For example, there is reason to believe that people with low self-esteem have greater difficulty trusting personal matters to another (though they are more easily convinced by persuaders with high status). We begin to catch the significance of this when we realize that shyness and low self-esteem go together, and these are both related to loneliness. Several studies complete the picture by showing that people who are most often lonely are the lowest risk-takers.

As children, some of us may have been exposed to parents or other people who promised things and then failed to keep their promises. If this happened to us enough, we probably found ourselves "demanding" considerably more proof of a partner's trustworthiness than someone who always had promises kept. Some of us may have had a relationship in which we disclosed very personal information, only to have it broadcast to others. One lady recently told me about an experience she had when a formerly close friend and she had a bad argument. Her former friend struck out at her by telling others confidences she had shared. The friend embellished the truth in order to make things look even worse. The relationship has never been restored, and the lady now finds it very difficult to get close to anyone.

We may come to see a person as trustworthy but still not disclose intimate information. Our willingness to become intimate is affected by the needs we feel, the potential benefit of risking compared to the cost of betrayal, the intimate relationships we already have available, and the opportunity there is to talk when needs arise. If we already have some close relationships, we may not feel compelled to deepen another one. If the need that we have is very risky, we may initially try to meet it individually. Some time ago I received a letter from a young man that I had never met. His letter was sent to me by a referral service. In it he disclosed that he had tried and failed for several years to cope with his sexual needs and wanted help in overcoming a strong habit of masturbation. His needs had finally shifted the cost of revealing himself to a lower level, although he still took a comparatively ''safe'' approach by writing to a professional he didn't know.

Assuming we are able to trust in a reasonably normal way, we will find ourselves slowly moving toward deeper relationships with those who meet our conditions of trustworthiness. One of the keys to going deeper is synchronizing. Synchronizing is simply the coordinated timing of our disclosures and forecasts about the relationship between us and our partner. I recently had the special treat of hearing Canadian duo pianists Mel and Holden Bowker play during a week of family camp. Our spirits were lifted with the beauty and magnificence of the music as it praised God. Part of the treat was also watching these two superb musicians playing complex, complementary arrangements with absolute precision. As their fingers flew up and down the keyboards, they occasionally glanced at each other and give a faint smile of approval. It was synchronization at its best. Their timing was virtually perfect as they meshed their individual expressions into beautiful harmony. When we develop a close relationship, it's important for us to realize we can't rush from superficial to intense and intimate disclosure. If we don't sense what our partner's pace is, we'll find one of two things happening. Either we'll move too fast and frighten our partner off, or we'll move too slowly and be perceived as unwilling to commit ourselves in a deeper way.

Synchronizing doesn't come easy. It not only involves evaluation, but it also trys to assess the intentions held by both us and our partner. It requires paying attention to very subtle verbal and nonverbal cues. If we sense uneasiness in either our partner or ourselves when we're revealing personal concerns, it's time to slow down. On the other hand, if he seems eager to spend time with us, listens attentively to our concerns, and initiates interaction, we've got a green light. Synchronizing is frequently a problem for people who are dating each other. I've had numerous individuals and couples come to me with the comment-question, "I'm not sure I'm ready to get married. How do I know if I'm really in love?" Usually this has been preceded by one of the pair signaling the desire for a deeper, long-range relationship at a time when the other partner isn't quite at the same spot. Such asynchrony usually stirs up a crisis and attempts to clarify just what each of their intentions and feelings are. In some cases, both are close enough so that the "slowpoke" is able to make the deeper commitment. At other times the pressure results in feelings of being "pushed," "suffocated," or "fenced in," and a breakup occurs. Once signals to move deeper have been sent out, it's usually very difficult to remain at the previous level of intimacy. Some couples decide, for example, that they'll "cool it" by dating others while continuing to see each other. They may also decide just to stop seeing each other for a period of time. These options rarely work because one or both partners see stepping back to a superficial relationship as artificial and emotionally unsatisfying. Often the person suggesting such backpedaling is viewed as untrustworthy from that point on.

Building intimacy also depends on building understanding. Understanding is built both by having common experiences and by talking more broadly and deeply about ourselves. As we reveal more about our basic values, our partner will be better able to piece together the underlying personality structure that shapes why and how we say and do things the way we do. As we move deeper in a relationship, however, it's also easier to misunderstand at the very time understanding is needed most. The misunderstanding often comes because we disclose ourselves partially, for fear of rejection, or act in ways which seem to contradict the image that our partner has constructed on the basis of interaction to that point. Feelings of anger and loneliness are generated by chronic misunderstanding. It's impossible, of course, for two people to perfectly understand each other. If we don't expect it, we won't be disillusioned.

There are five communication skills, however, which will facilitate understanding.[3] The first is to be aware of our own feelings and thoughts so that we don't communicate muddled messages. Misunderstanding often arises because we don't allow ourselves to clearly articulate how we feel, what our desires are, what we see or hear, and what we're thinking. The result is that we convey messages that confuse our partner. Second, we need to check out or clarify our partner's communication. This involves clearly stating what we have seen or heard and asking for clarification so that we don't misinterpret. We must make sure that we communicate the desire to be accurate. We should also ask our partner to feed back what he's heard when we give some particularly sensitive information. Third, we should allow proper time and establish a place conducive to discussion when we need to communicate complex matters or clear up a misunderstanding. Fourth, we must avoid a confrontational style of communication that demands, accuses, and reacts — it will only establish a defensive cycle of interaction. We have to believe our partner is trying to understand us rather than seeing him as an enemy if he disagrees with something we've said. Finally, we must affirm our partner and ourselves. We must not put either our partner or ourselves down by denying the value of what has been revealed, by saying things like, "You don't care" or "You just don't understand." And avoid getting into a win-lose situation when there's disagreement. Instead we must each try to help our partner to understand, and be willing to compromise. Steer clear of blaming, self-defense, and ridicule. We can give each other the benefit of the doubt and try to verbally affirm our partner's intentions while we work through our disagreement. Attachment occurs and deepens as a result of affirmation. For the infant, affirmation comes from being held and having basic biological needs cared for. For teens and adults, it comes from feeling valued, accepted, and being shown affection through words, actions, and touch.

That Special One

For most of us marriage holds the greatest possibility of a deeply intimate emotional and physical relationship. How is intimacy built in marriage? For the most part intimate marriages develop in the same way that other close relationships do. The obvious differences are that in marriage we are known more completely than in any other relationship, and we are able to express ourselves sexually.

Intimate marriage begins by laying the right foundation. Those of us who have watched construction of a skyscraper know that considerable time is spent digging a huge, deep hole in which the base of the building is laid. I have heard that skyscraper foundations may be as deep as half the height of the above-ground portion. If you've ever tried to remove a tall tree, you've discovered that the roots run almost inextricably deep and wide into the ground. The foundations of skyscrapers and trees allow them to stand without toppling in the midst of great winds and earthquakes. It should come as no surprise that, as a group, those who have the longest engagements have the most-stable marriages. We seem to be geared to microwave marriages — date somebody for a few months, feel passionate, and get married. Some people get married so fast it's no wonder they feel like they've married a stranger! At some point we ought to start paying attention to the divorce statistics and realize that short and sensual just doesn't work as a prelude for satisfying, intimate marriages.

If you're considering marriage, don't rush into it. Take time to get to know one another. Share a variety of experiences, and talk about things that matter. Most contemporary dating is aimed at presenting a carefully cultivated positive impression. If you want to be sure of a good marriage, you need to get beyond the game-playing of looking good to being able to reveal the not-so-perfect parts of yourselves. You need to get to a point where you can each see how you handle conflicts. *Then* you'll be ready to tie a knot that won't come loose with the first few jolts of reality.

Does that mean that you shouldn't feel a romantic tingle toward your prospective mate? Not at all. A little romance and heart flutter is only natural. You *should* respond differently than you would toward a box of rolled oats. I'm not for drab, problem-centered courtships. The point is that you shouldn't spend all of your time cultivating the sensual. Let's face it — our initial attraction to a prospective mate is usually physical. We like the way she or he looks! There's nothing wrong with that. You don't have to date only "ugly" people to be sure your motives are right. It's also normal to want to express your affection physically. Up to a point (short of heavy petting and intercourse) that may be okay. But if physical pleasure becomes your focus, you're building on sand. You'll find yourself starry-eyed and "madly in love," but once the temperature goes down, you may think you must have been mad to get hooked into marriage with your partner. The feelings which you interpreted as "love" are more likely to have been camouflaged feelings or fear of loneliness.

Many people use marriage as an escape from loneliness. One woman told me that she and her husband got married because they were lonely. Now, five years later, she feels lonelier than ever and has landed in the hospital several times with emotional and physical difficulties stemming from her unhappy marriage.

I marvel that we have to go through a more stringent test to get a driver's license than we do to get married or have kids. Every year over a million people become the victims of divorce. About 65 percent of all the people who are married have substantial problems. Does this mean that marriage is to blame? Some think so and argue for alternative forms of relationship that involve little or no commitment. It seems to me that superficial dating and courting patterns are what need to be altered. We need to make it tougher for people to live together rather than easier.

Solid and intimate marriages are built on compatibility. The time to learn about compatibility is prior to marriage, not after. There are at least three aspects of compatibility that need to be considered.[4] The first is the match between fundamental personality characteristics. A good fit on this level is crucial if a marriage is to be satisfying and solid. No two people will ever be completely compatible. The better the match, however, the more likely the relationship will last. Being aware of incompatible areas may also help each partner make allowances and satisfactorily tolerate each other's differences. Included in this match are: sociability, emotional stability, dominance, intellectual capacity, sexual needs, and energy levels. Let's look briefly at each of these aspects of basic compatibility.

People differ in their *need for people*. If we have a strong need for people, we may *have* to be around others much of the time. If our partner doesn't have such a need, strong tensions may develop. One of us may like quiet evenings at home, while the other just *has* to have people over or go out to events where they can mingle and talk. If we aren't able to work out a compromise, our marriage may be filled with contention. If we like to go out, and do so, our spouse may feel deserted and unloved. Or suspicions may develop about the "goer's" motivation for being gone; accusations of infidelity can crop up. Being apart much of the time simply doesn't give us the time we need to talk and build a sense of companionship.

If one or both of you has *emotional problems*, you need to be aware. Recently I had opportunity to meet two engaged people who had asked for prayer and counseling. Both the man and woman seemed agitated, stared a great deal, were very self-focused, and told about how anxious and insecure they felt. The man reported that he had heard voices talking to him. All of the symptoms suggested that he was psychotic and she was deeply neurotic. The likelihood of their marriage working is less than zero because they are both so full of inner conflict that they are barely able to function on a practical level, much less develop the give and take of an intimate relationship. If you or your partner seems to be withdrawn from reality, has hallucinations, or gives other indications of deep emotional disturbance, *don't* marry. The same is true with regard to heavy drinking or drug use. Stay away from marriage. Many people suffer from less severe instability, called neuroses. If you or your partner has chronic feelings of anxiety, frequent fears, periodic (recurrent) depression, deep feelings of inferiority, or a tendency to turn stresses into physical ailments, you are likely to have considerable ups and downs in your marriage. This doesn't mean your marriage won't work. It can. But it will require a great deal of patience and understanding. If you're aware of problems ahead of marriage, discuss them with your prospective mate and be willing to commit yourself to professional therapy. Having said all of this, let me mention that emotional ups and downs are normal. We all have them. They're usually event-oriented (e.g., loss of a job; death of someone close). Usually with love from our spouse and other close friends, and some time, we get back on top. Our patterns are ones of stability, marked by occasional difficulties, though, and not ones of instability with brief periods of stability.

Another aspect of basic compatibility is *dominance*. It used to be that males were automatically expected to call the shots. That is no longer so. Even in contemporary Christian marriage, determining who makes the decisions is not cut-and-dried. Most Christians agree that the husband should have final authority in some areas at least, but they also feel that the wife should be listened to with respect and should be the decision-maker in areas of her major responsibilities or special competence. The problem is complicated when, because of personality differences, a wife is very dominant while the husband is more passive, or when both partners are dominant. Simply saying that the wife should always submit to the dictates of her husband on all matters seems to be inadequate — it sells her needs and competencies short. On the other hand, arguing for individual rights seems destined to create an irresolvable power struggle, especially when both partners are dominant. The best match is probably when one is more dominant and the other less. The biblical match seems to deal more with responsibility than dominance. It suggests that the husband is like the president of a corporation with "final" authority, while the wife can be a highly competent and vigorous vice-president who is listened to with respect and who respects the choices of the president. As in a business, both are under the ultimate authority of the board (God). Also, as in a business, certain responsibilities and decisions are left entirely up to the vice-president. The board and executive officers meet to determine and evaluate policies and procedures on a regular basis. In contemporary marriage, exact spheres of responsibility usually have to be negotiated, not simply assumed. Unless both partners are aware of each other's dominance needs and able to coordinate them, there is great likelihood that the marriage will be full of strife.

Unless spouses are reasonably compatible *intellectually*,

problems can arise also. First, people who are substantially
different in intellectual capacity will find it difficult to plan
together or talk together. Usually it leads to a lack of respect,
cutting remarks, and pulling back from communication with the
"inferior" partner. Second, it may lead to an unhealthy search
for a third person who can understand and communicate on
levels that the intellectually "superior" partner needs. Many
extramarital affairs and divorces have originated because one of
the partners felt the need to relate to someone who was an
intellectual equal, who could give and take and understand. It's
usually more workable in our society, if the partners are fairly
comparable, for the man to be intellectually more competent.
Though this is rapidly changing, men are still usually looked to
for primary employment and success. Intelligence elevates his
chances of occupational success. Also, perhaps due to culture,
women are generally happier if they can look up to their husbands rather than down. Ideally, of course, partners should be
roughly comparable in general intelligence, with somewhat
similar intellectual interests and complementary intellectual skills
(one may be great in mechanical intelligence, another in logical
reasoning). That is why it's usually better for college grads to
marry college grads, high school grads to marry high school
grads. The chances for intellectual compatibility are greater.

Another aspect of basic compatibility is the need for *sexual
expression*. Some have pushed this into major prominence and
then justified various forms of premarital cohabitation on the
premise of better marital adjustment. Differences in the strength
of sexual drive change, however, as a function of age and life
situation. There are some biologically based patterns — the sex
drive of men usually peaks in the early twenties, while women
peak in their late twenties. Because women tend to marry older
men, this can create some tensions. Some people have a very
strong sexual drive, others much weaker. Most so-called sexual
incompatibility is a function of attitudes, however. Even in the
case of mismatched sex drives, a marriage can be very happy if

the oversexed partner is willing to partially sublimate his or her needs, and the undersexed partner is willing to adjust his or her natural level of satisfaction. In cases of frigidity, impotence, and preference differences, professional counseling and patience by the nontroubled partner can usually overcome difficulties. It is crucial to remember that sexual satisfaction is largely related to happiness in the general relationship; it doesn't stand alone. Sexual differences that originate within marriages are simply an indication of the emotional health of the partnership.

Basic compatibility also includes the factor of *energy levels*. People vary in the amount of energy they have available. One friend of mine goes like a ''house afire'' and seems to require only four or five hours of sleep each night. Others drag out of bed tired after eight hours of sleep and need an afternoon nap. (Sometimes lethargy can be due to emotional upset, including loneliness, but it also can be due to biological need.) A person with lower energy levels will be content with, indeed need, fewer activities than a dynamo. The dynamo may be constantly taking on new challenges and find something always demanding his attention. Tension can develop if there is energy incompatibility. One spouse may resent his or her partner going to bed earlier (or later), the need the dynamo has to always be doing something and not taking time just to talk, or the ''laziness'' of the low-energy spouse.

Finally, there is *spiritual compatibility*. Countless Christians have tried to bypass this dimension by marrying non-Christians they thought they could ''win to the Lord.'' In most cases this doesn't happen. This is because for a genuine Christian, faith is more than just belief. Rather, it is a way of life which affects feelings, plans, decisions, and actions. The born-again Christian who marries a non-Christian finds that he can't have communion at the very core of who he is and what makes him tick. The marriage may survive, but only at the cost of deep loneliness for the believer. Spiritual compatibility includes consideration of whether both partners are ''born again,'' what priority seeking God's guidance and serving Him has in comparison with other values, how important prayer and Bible-reading are, what place the "filling of the Spirit" and speaking in tongues has in their lives, what their beliefs and behaviors are with regard to commitment to a church body, their view of God, how they include God in daily and long-range decisions, and what kind of worship styles they find most satisfying. Spouses who vary significantly on these items will find themselves restricted in their communication. The differences tend to be intensified when decisions regarding children and religious upbringing have to be made.

In addition to basic compatibility, background factors (age, religion, socioeconomic status, education) need to mesh as much as possible. There is also a growth compatibility, which really can't be charted ahead of time. This compatibility really comes about as each partner shows respect, reveals himself, and affirms the other through the many experiences they have together. It is really another term for intimacy, which is built on the principles we have already mentioned.

Our discussion of basic compatibility is meant to highlight some of the dimensions that have proved important for stable, satisfying marriage. It is recommended that couples who are dating seriously consider taking the Taylor-Johnson Temperament Analysis or The Marriage Compatibility Inventory[5] under the supervision of a trained pastor or counselor. They provide a better basis for knowing if there is basic compatibility or conflict between personalities. If the test indicates incompatibility, it's best to reconsider continuing the relationship, despite your feelings. It can provide a constructive agenda for further courtship and a head start on building a strong marriage. You'll be better able to understand each other, articulate your needs, and deal with your differences.

Beyond compatibility, marital intimacy requires *commitment*. Commitment is simply the willingness to persevere. It's the keeping of one's promise, regardless of the reasons to renege.

Marital commitment, "till death do us part," is an act of faith and unconditional love. Interestingly, some of the very same humanists who cry for unconditional love also advocate trial cohabitation (in the name of freedom). Trial cohabitation is *conditional* love! When two people agree to live together and have physical intimacy to see if they're "compatible," they advocate partial commitment. In order for marriage to fully flower into intimacy, there must be the genuine, stated intention to stick it out. That doesn't mean everybody will, but failure to persevere is no reason to do away with public commitment. Indeed, the marriage ritual aids couples not to abandon ship at the first sign of a storm, in part because of the public witness that family and friends have had of their commitment. Genuine commitment provides a base of security that allows greater freedom without fear of abandonment. It's not a bad idea to explore each other's views of what commitment means, and of divorce, prior to marriage.

Within marriage it is vitally important to *accentuate the positive*. At first that's not too hard. As time goes on, though, we begin to notice things in our spouse we may not like. The adventurous antics we once found exhilarating may begin to seem childish. The air of confidence and assertiveness that we found reassuring may begin to seem like arrogance and manipulation. The agreeability and submissiveness which made the relationship easy at first may begin to look more like lack of intelligence or take on subtle traces of hostility. It's vitally important that we expect to find imperfections and set our wills at the outset to pay attention to the things we like. If we set about trying to change our partner or expect him or her not to have faults, we'll start a cycle of criticism and defensiveness that will raise barriers.

Get in the habit of regularly complimenting each other. This helps us to keep focusing on what we like. Author Charlie Shedd tells about the commitment he and his wife, Martha, made to each other thirty years ago. Each day they give each other a genuine, verbal compliment. As he puts it, it takes some creativity, but it's well worth it. A few days after I heard Charlie, I listened to another speaker aim some pointed put-downs at his wife in the form of jokes. What a difference! Charlie cherished his wife with compliments; the other speaker used his wife for laughs. I've no doubt which is the happier and deeper marriage.

Another way to help accentuate the positive is to get into the habit of doing enjoyable things together. Many couples get so caught up in the demands of work and family life that they neglect play times together. Our times of enjoyment should command as much priority as our most important business engagements. One couple I know takes nightly walks in a park overlooking the ocean, another gets season tickets for the opera, another has a weekly date for a sundae, and another plays tennis together. If possible, do this with just the two of you — try swapping babysitting with someone else if you're short on funds. If that's not possible, take the kids along, but help them understand this is primarily Mom and Dad's time. Times of fun together help us get through the more serious times because they provide us with a picture of someone we find enjoyable to be with. Good times help us to build a reservoir of positives to cover the negatives.

Avoid blaming and criticizing your partner. One of the surest ways to help a marriage go sour and to see your partner put up walls of self-protection is blaming. Inevitably things go wrong — a train will be missed, a prized dish will break, the wrong-sized container will be bought, a poor investment will be made, and so forth. Disappointments can either be accepted with an attitude of "We both did our best. Next time I know things will go better because we've both learned," and "I know it was an accident, and I'm really disappointed but it'll be okay," or "What's the matter with you? Can't you ever do anything right? I knew I should've done it myself. You blow it every time." The former responses express love and acceptance in the midst of disappointment. They draw spouses together. The latter drive them apart. Few of us can stand to be blamed without feeling alienated and unloved. After a while, couples can slide into a pattern of attack and defense that completely crowds out affection and intimacy. The scriptural injunction, ''Do not judge, or you too will be judged. For in the same way you judge others, you will be judged, and with the measure you use, it will be measured to you'' (Matthew 7:1-2), is all too true in marriage. Relationships tend to operate on the principle of reciprocity. What we give is what we get. If we start giving negative feedback to our spouse, we can be fairly sure, but for the grace of God and the maturity of the spouse, that we'll get the same back.

This is why forgiveness is such a vital tool in marriage. Practice forgiving long before marriage. The best forgiveness in a marriage is the kind that is given before it is asked. If we require our spouse to ask our forgiveness, to admit he or she is wrong before we'll grant it, we're using our tool as a bludgeon. Love prompts us to forgive *before* we're asked, and even if we're not asked. Instant forgiveness allows us the grace to respond to disappointments and hurts without blame or attack. If we have a hard time doing this, we should recall the times we've done things that have hurt but have been forgiven. It is also sobering to think about Christ's forgiveness of us even though our sin sent Him to the cross. If we continually have problems forgiving others, it may mean that we are very insecure ourselves.

Granting forgiveness is only part of the picture, however. We also need to be willing and prompt to admit when we're wrong and ask forgiveness. If you're the kind of person who is always right, remember Proverbs 16:2: ''All a man's ways seem innocent to him, but motives are weighed by the Lord.'' We may appear to get away with things at first. But after a while we'll start noticing that our spouse seems resentful ''for no reason,'' or seems to withdraw. Steamrolling our partner to get our own way accomplishes only two things: It crushes our partner's sense of worth and takes the life out of our marriage. People who have difficulty asking forgiveness also betray an underlying sense of low self-esteem. They find it painful to see themselves as they really are. If marriage is to deepen, we've got to be ready to admit our wrongs and genuinely ask our partner for forgiveness. The same goes for our parents when they wrong their children, also. Some of the rebellion and bitterness we see by kids toward their parents comes from an unwillingness by parents to humble themselves and ask forgiveness when they've been too harsh or said something wrong or unkind.

One of the keys to building marital intimacy is *learning the language of love*.[6] Just saying "I love you" isn't enough. Don't misunderstand me. Words of endearment are vitally important. I've met a number of women who long to hear a simple "I love you" from their husbands. Typically the husband says, "Of course I love her, can't she tell? I'm married to her and bring home the bacon, don't I?" Both men and women need to be told they're loved. But we need more than just words. Words have to be supported by actions that our spouse interprets as being motivated by love. Each of us has a special language we need to hear. Touch, time together for talking, meeting material needs, willingly doing the house or yard work, special notes, an occasional lunch together, praying together, sexual tenderness, and a host of other actions can speak love depending on our respective backgrounds. Part of getting to know each other is learning what speaks to your spouse. Often timing is crucial. If you buy roses for your wife and take her out to dinner, only to announce that you've decided to go on a week's hunting trip (and you know she doesn't like to stay alone), you've blown it. In her mind the roses and dinner will probably be seen as a bribe rather than an expression of love. Surprises like notes or cards on nonbirthday or anniversary times are usually seen as expressions of love if they're not linked in time with an argument or request. Part of the adventure of a growing relationship is learning to say "I love you" in language your spouse understands.

Intimacy grows as each partner nurtures the other. This includes a willingness to encourage, allowing each other freedom to grow

as individuals as well as agreeing on limits of freedom. As you
nurture each other and build each other up, you'll also find that
you can interrupt negative response cycles more quickly. It's
important to realize that every marriage has cycles of intimacy.[7]
There are times when you will feel very close and times when
you feel distant or in conflict. This is normal, not a sign that you
don't love each other. By continuing to think the best about your
partner when you're in the "anti-intimacy" phase of the cycle,
as well as building deep satisfaction at the other times, you'll be
better able to avoid getting into a negative tailspin that becomes
a pattern of alienation and conflict.

One of the most critical things for us to learn is how to
constructively handle anger. Everybody feels angry at some
point in a close relationship. Anger usually reflects a feeling of
betrayal, frustration, or disappointment. It tells us something is
wrong. Paul encourages us to "be angry and sin not" (Ephesians
4:26). That suggests that anger itself is not usually the problem
(unless it reveals a pattern of deeper, chronic hostility), but how
we express it. Expressed in the wrong way it can ruin marriages.
Nonconstructive expressions include ridicule, physical abuse,
throwing things, not talking with each other, screaming, and
swearing directed at your partner. The original discussion tends
to get lost, and partners often get locked into insulting and name
calling. Focusing on a partner's "bad" anger may result in even
greater anger!

There are constructive ways to handle anger.[8] The first is to
establish some means of signaling to our partner that we're
getting upset. Have a standard procedure that both agree on —
maybe it's just saying, "I'm getting angry," or "I've got to take
a walk, let's talk a little later." The best thing to do is to
temporarily separate. The immediate intensity of angry feelings
normally lessens in a short period of time. Doing something
physical — lifting weights, walking, running, scrubbing the
floor — can calm us down.

Then we should try to successfully work through our anger in an imaginary conversation with our spouse, and picture ourselves expressing our feelings without abuse. If our anger was stirred by an action that can't be called back, there's no sense in berating — that won't change the act — though it will change our relationship. Our partner should be given the benefit of the doubt. He or she probably feels worse than we do.

Finally, try talking together. Before you start again, try kneeling down and praying together. Listen carefully to your spouse. If you're having a disagreement, consciously feel yourself trying to see things from his or her point of view. Be honest with yourself and make sure that your anger isn't just an expression of self-centeredness. Don't allow yourself to start an internal response of criticizing and blaming or you'll find yourself angry again. Allow time to talk about the issue. Don't rush things. Some people start talking about sensitive issues ten minutes before they have to leave for work; that's guaranteed to lead to an explosion and unresolved conflict. Also try to pick a good time of day to talk. Usually people are fresher and more in control of their emotions in the early part of the day, after a night's rest. If that's so, try not to get started on touchy issues late at night when emotions are apt to be more volatile. If our partner is angry, block out the anger and listen to what's really being said. Try to show understanding. If we've done something wrong, we should apologize and genuinely ask forgiveness. If our partner says things that hurt, try to remember they are being said in anger. By asking God to calm us we won't return anger for anger — we'll respond in love.

Finally, the road to deep marital intimacy involves *learning to share our spiritual lives*. Perhaps one of the hardest things for a couple to do is to get on their knees together in prayer. In some ways it is one of the most vulnerable positions we can be in, if we genuinely open our hearts to God. Such praying binds couples together in a special way, however, as they communicate deep feelings, desires, requests, and praise. Regularly studying the Bible together, or discussing things that God has shown us, also builds intimacy. Many couples establish spiritual goals at the beginning of a new year; they may covenant to seek God to use them in bringing a certain person or number of people to Christ, or plan together how to witness for Christ with their neighbors. Trusting God together to meet specific needs will strengthen our bond with Him while it sustains and nourishes the marriage relationship.

10
OVERCOMING LOSS

osing a close relationship is one of the most difficult experiences we face. We feel angry, guilty, cheated, and
depressed. People describe themselves as feeling a deep void or
inner emptiness. We feel abandoned and helpless, much like the
toddler whose parents leave him with a babysitter for the first
time.

Inevitably, we feel lonely. We may try to deny our loneliness
and push it out of our consciousness, but that doesn't get rid of
it. If we suppress it, it will only come out in other, more subtle
ways. There is no healthy way to completely escape the pain of
grief and loneliness that loss triggers. The more intimate the
relationship was, the more pain we can expect to feel. There are
ways to *lessen* the loneliness of loss, but not to remove it. We'll
look at some of those ways in this chapter.

There are many events that we may experience as loss. Some
suggest that loss is any event that brings change into a predictable
environment.[1] They suggest that such things as the birth of a
baby (loss of freedom), the earning of a promotion (loss of
former network), and finishing a Ph.D. (loss of academic setting
and advisor-student relationship) produce some of the same
depression and grief as losing a loved one. It's clear that loss

does involve a break from the past and ushers in uncertainty. In this chapter I have restricted our consideration of loss to mobility, divorce, death, and retirement. Each of these events causes a break from the past. Memories take the place of interaction. Although the break is not necessarily permanent in the cases of moving, divorce, and retirement, there is a fundamental change in the nature of our relationship. In a very real sense there is no recovery of what was before. The process of interaction changes. There is no longer the daily dialogue and sharing of experiences which gave our relationship its uniqueness. In all cases of loss, a part of our very identity that was created and maintained by our relationship is sealed off. In some ways we can say that a part of oneself dies in the process of loss.

As close relationships develop, regular patterns of interaction are established. We know that our partner will respond in consistent ways to various situations. We learn to adjust our ways of doing things, taking each other into account. We actually take on some of our partner's characteristics. As a result, our world takes on a special kind of predictability and security. When loss comes our world changes. If our partner has died, we no longer have him to turn to for advice; we're on our own for decisions; there is no one who looks, talks, or does things quite the same way.

If we have moved, divorced, or retired, our world also changes. The old patterns of communication no longer hold. This is especially true when divorce is involved. Drawn-out court proceedings often redefine us and our former mate as enemies. In all instances of loss, we have a feeling of standing alone, not knowing quite what to do, and not being able to turn to a familiar face for assistance.

It is natural for us to try to recover a lost relationship. At first we'll probably find ourselves thinking a great deal about our partner. We may think that we hear his voice, or find ourselves starting to ask him a question. But no one is there. Some try to reestablish contact with deceased loved ones through mediums (this is definitely forbidden by Scripture). Others try to recover their relationship by treating another person in the same way as they did the lost one. For example, parents who have lost a child through death may have another child and try to make him into a carbon copy of the lost one. Some who have lost a spouse through death or divorce remarry too quickly, while still in the grieving process. Often this leads to tragedy, unless they have had a long-standing friendship with the new spouse. Loneliness is *never* a good reason for marriage.

The first thing to remember when facing loss is that *we will never find another person to duplicate the one we've lost.* Don't try. Things will never be exactly the same. Painful as this is to accept, failure to accept it is likely to launch us into a tragic round of frantic activity and frustrated relationships. This *doesn't* mean that we should avoid other close relationships or never get married again. But we must be fair to new friends — we can't expect them to do things the same way, respond to us in the familiar pattern, laugh at the same things as our lost partner, or think and feel in the same way. Every relationship is unique. Focus on those aspects of other people that you can enjoy and appreciate. Realize that every person has a storehouse of treasures if you are willing to develop bonds with him, and don't require all treasures to be identical.

Sometimes people go to the opposite extreme. They accept the fact that they can't replace a lost relationship and therefore don't want anyone to fill the void. They prefer to live with memories. Often they'll inflate their lost loved one so much that all others seem pallid by comparison. For some this may work because the opportunity to develop substitute companionship is very limited. Older widows and widowers may find memories a genuine and effective comfort. For most, however, this kind of thinking prevents development of new relationships and prolongs loneliness. Often the refusal to develop new intimacy stems from a sense of loyalty or guilt about the lost one. In cases of death particularly, we need to realize that the deceased one's

feelings won't be hurt in the slightest. It's probably a wise thing
to talk about this remarriage prior to illness or death of a spouse
to get feelings worked out. Usually a spouse does not want the
remaining one to be bound to a memory, but for him or her to be
free to develop life from that point.

Second, we must *be prepared to feel lonely* when we lose
close relationships. The amount of loneliness we feel will vary
with the kind of loss and the amount of intimacy we had. For
example, it is likely that we'll feel less loneliness if we or our
friend moves than if our friend (spouse) dies. If we've been
married forty-five years, we'll feel more lonely than if we were
married five years. Loneliness is less crippling if we're willing
to face it. This will help us to take constructive steps to lessen it
in the longer run.

Third, we need to *avoid self-pity*. Probably nothing intensifies
and prolongs loneliness more than self-pity. Self-pity is another
way of saying, "I don't deserve this, and I can't do anything
about it." It's sophisticated pouting. Self-pity paralyzes initiative. When we feel sorry for ourselves, we get so wrapped up in
our sad situation that we're likely to do nothing to improve it. It's
something like the old dog who sat on a thorn and proceeded to
mournfully howl in agony. When his owner came along and
asked him why he didn't get up, the dog replied that it felt too
good to howl. Well-meaning listeners who encourage self-
pitiers to continually recite their woes after an initial period of
mourning really only dig a deeper hole for them. Self-pity is an
excuse for avoiding responsibility. The truth of the matter is that
there is much in life that we can't explain and from our perspective "don't deserve." If we indulge in self-pity, we are announc-
ing that we are helpless before the fate that uncontrollably assails
us. It's often true that we have no control over loss events, but it's
not true that we are helpless. We are able to respond in a variety
of ways to the experience of loss. Self-pity also drives us further
into depression because it looks only at the bad things happening
and refuses to look for a silver lining. It promotes loneliness

because of the total self-preoccupation involved — there's no
time or energy left to be concerned about others. Our self-
centeredness will simply drive others off after a while, and we'll
find ourselves even more intensely alone. We must set our will
against self-pity. As soon as possible, we should begin helping
others in need. It will allow us to get the attention off ourselves.
And remember that ultimately God will cause things to work out
for our best, *if* we let Him.

Moving

When you move, one of the first things to consider is the type
of neighborhood you want to live in. This is vitally important for
everybody's emotional well-being. Take the time you need to
adequately assess areas of the community. If necessary, rent for
a few months. As much as possible, try to locate a neighborhood
similar to the one you've been in (unless that didn't meet your
needs or you expect your family situation to change). If you're a
wife not working outside of your home, try to find a neighborhood where there are a number of women at home during the
day. If you have children, try to locate an area with children
roughly the same age as your own. When exploring for a place to
live, don't hesitate to ask those already living there about such
matters and about how stable the neighborhood seems to be. If
there's a lot of change, consider picking a more stable area so all
the kids you thought would be there for your own to play with
aren't likely to be gone in six months. Many people find that
buying a house similar in layout and appearance to their former
house helps them to feel more as though they "belong."

Take the initiative in developing new friendships. Invite the
neighbor kids over to play and the adults over for tea or dessert.
It's usually best to concentrate on one neighbor (or family) at a
time. Offer to take care of their pets if they're going on vacation.
Join the PTA if you have kids in school, and try to get on a
smaller committee. If you are a Christian, become active in a
local church. Do more than just attend the formal Sunday

morning service. You'll get to know people a lot faster if you also attend the smaller Sunday evening and midweek prayer services. Invite someone you think you'd like to know better over for popcorn after the evening service. Volunteer to help in various activities. Reach out to people who may be in need. It's usually helpful if you can meet and become friends with someone else who is also new to the area. This gives you someone who is likely to understand the many mixed feelings you may have your first year and someone to explore the community with as you look for stores, churches, and schools. Don't be surprised, however, if that relationship ends up being a short-term one. That's okay, for in the unsettled period you've been of mutual help. If you've mainly related to each other because of your mutual newness, it's likely you'll find yourselves making other, more intimate relationships as time goes on and you get to know people better.

Try not to be critical of people or programs in your new community. Also, remember that such a comparison really isn't fair because you haven't had time to get to know and enjoy your new acquaintances. Organizations and churches will do things differently, also. We usually favor the familiar because it makes us feel secure. Try to be open to the new procedures and philosophies. Try to learn and adjust rather than judging and closing yourself off. Make a habit of regularly saying out loud the things you *like* about your new house, new neighborhood, new school, new church, and new acquaintances. Consciously avoid talking about dislikes.

Realize that for a period of time you will have to endure being an "outsider." People won't seek your advice, drop by to talk, or relate to you as those who wept at your leaving did. But also remember that neither at first did the people where you used to live. Be optimistic. Realize that it may take twelve to eighteen months to become an "insider" in a group of friends, but that it will happen if you reach out to others and take initiative. As time goes on, people will start returning your invitations. The word will get out that you're really a special person worth getting to know.

If you made your decision to move in response to God's specific leading, you can also turn to Him. For example, my wife and I felt a need for new friends (one or two couples) who would also hit it off well with our three boys. We made this one of our prayer requests and experienced the developing of a new relationship that surprised and delighted us. In the spaces while you're still getting settled you can also turn to the Lord and tell Him very specifically what your needs are, asking for special fellowship through His Spirit. The Scripture promises us that as we draw near to God, He comes close to us (James 4:8) and helps satisfy our inner needs.

Death and Divorce

In both divorce and death there is a very similar grieving process.[2] This is especially true in cases of suddenly announced divorce, and for the partner who didn't initiate it. We refer to both those who have been divorced or have lost a loved one by death as "mourners," "grievers," or "bereaved." At first there is *shock and disbelief*. Emotions overwhelm, and bizarre behaviors (such as laughing inappropriately) may occur. Everything inside the griever tries to block out the bad news. It may seem like a bad dream, but there's no waking up. During this initial state it's important for consolers just to be physically present and to listen. Don't try to give pearls of advice or comfort someone with religious orthodoxy. Just be there and love.

As the news sinks in, the bereaved may either become hysterical or withdraw and escape. After a while the grief of loss is felt in *disorganization*. The bereaved seem confused and even feel out of touch with reality. Sometimes they feel like bystanders, watching things happen in a detached way. They desperately need someone whom they can trust to be with them and to hug, hold their hand, or give them a shoulder to cry on. They need to be encouraged to cry and to talk until they can begin to make sense out of their confusion.

In the third state, there is often an *unleashing of emotions*. The hurt, helplessness, and frustration they are feeling deep within may burst out in unsocial monologues and anger. The anger may be directed at the lost love, at other family members, or at a counselor or doctor. Unless these feelings are allowed expression, it is likely they will simmer and express themselves in the future in depression, migraine headaches, and ulcers. Helpers need to affirm the griever and show him that they accept him in spite of his outbursts. Usually the griever is ashamed of himself and needs special support.

The fourth stage of experience is *guilt*. There is a concentration on the good that could have been, and desire for another try. Usually there is a turning over and over in the mind of things that could have been done to prevent the death or divorce. Often there is self-deprecation and difficulty in accepting oneself. Listeners can help most by being assuring and accepting.

Next there is a *sense of loss and loneliness*. Usually this doesn't hit right away. More frequently it comes after the ending ritual (funeral or divorce) has taken place and sympathizing family and friends have returned to their own routines. Even in unhappy marriages there is a bond that loss breaks. What was taken for granted is suddenly highlighted and treasured. Loneliness must be allowed to "bottom out" if grief is to run to a healthy completion. If it is fully felt there will be movement to *relief*. Relief is simply a release from the pain of seeing a relationship die, from the practical stresses of bills and court proceedings, from the uncertainties and the loss. A confidante who can relate to this release will help free the mourner from feelings of guilt.

Finally, most grievers reach the stage of *reestablishment*, where hope gradually replaces despair, new love softens the

loss, and the griever begins to look outward again. Reestablishment should be allowed to come at the griever's own pace.

Because the responses to death and divorce are so similar, a
number of suggestions for coping with the loneliness of loss
apply to both. There are three differences, however, that need to
be pointed out. These differences make the loneliness of divorce
somewhat more difficult than that of death. First, divorce carries
with it a sense of no finality. There is usually the need to
continue relating to the former spouse if there are children
involved. Though there is grief, there is often no permanent
good-bye. Instead there is the constant reminder of what might
have been and the intimacy that once was there every time the
former spouses meet. Though the partner is there and one's heart
may yearn for restoration, for many there can be none. The sense
of isolation and loneliness deepens further if one's former spouse
remarries. That is the final rejection.

The feelings of personal rejection that the partner who is
divorced typically faces also distinguish death and divorce.
Except in cases of suicide, a partner's death doesn't carry a
message of rejection. Divorce inevitably does. One has been
known intimately and extensively and has been found wanting.
Divorced Christians may also feel condemned and rejected by
God. This is especially true in churches that consider divorce an
inexcusable sin. These feelings of rejection are why it is so
crucial for divorced people to create a new role where they can
feel accepted for who they are. Pastors, family, and friends have
a vitally important part to play in showing love and acceptance,
in conveying that the divorced person is worthwhile and still
wanted.

Spouses also tend to lose their marriage partners by death
later in life than those who are divorced. The fact that spouse
death tends to occur later creates special circumstances that
widows especially must face if they have not learned a variety of
life management skills. Widowers may actually end up more

lonely than widows if they have not learned to develop satisfying social relations that they can maintain on their own. Though older widowers have more latitude in marrying, they are likely to have fewer options of developing close friends of the same sex. For one thing, men die earlier and there are fewer to choose from. For another, men in American society have generally not learned how to simply enjoy talking to other men without some kind of external purpose or work structure. For men, talk is commonly viewed as a means to an end. For women, it is more likely to be enjoyed in itself, or at most as a means of deepening a friendship. Exceptions to this pattern may be found in certain ethnic groups which have institutionalized male companionship for older men through lawn bowling and similar activities.

Coping With Death and Divorce

In spite of these differences, I'd like to suggest some guidelines that will help those suffering from divorce or the death of a loved one to more effectively cope with grief and loneliness.

1. *Don't deny your feelings* or your grief. Face up to anger, anxiety, guilt, bitterness, rejection, and loneliness. As you take responsibility for your feelings, realize that they are part of adjusting to your loss. Don't think of yourself as inadequate or a "poor" Christian witness. If you try to cover up and act as if you're totally in control so others won't be embarrassed, you'll only intensify your loneliness. Don't allow yourself to feel ashamed or childish. You're not childish. In ancient biblical times people wept, moaned, and tore their hair at a publicly accepted place — the wailing wall in Jerusalem. By getting their feelings out in this socially acceptable way they were spared deeper, prolonged depression. Talk out your feelings with someone you can trust. Talk about your lost partner, about your grief, anger, and feelings of abandonment.

Talking helps to clarify what has happened and what must be done. Also, act out your grief.[3] Again, the ancient world encouraged tearing one's clothes or putting ashes on one's head. We might do well to reconsider this kind of expression. Other ways to express grief are to wear mourning clothes for a period of time or to fast. Should funerals be jubilant, lighthearted affairs? At times they may appropriately be so, if the remaining spouse or the deceased wished it that way. This is probably most natural and appropriate in cases where there has been time to prepare for death, acceptance has been achieved by both the dying person and the one left, and a real sense of God's victory has been experienced. We must also be careful not to turn aside the grief of bereaved people with pat responses — ''Just turn it over to Jesus and it'll be okay!'' or ''Trust in Jesus and praise Him and you won't be lonely!'' Surely these things will help. Jesus invites us to come in our need, and He responds. But He has also made us to need love and comfort from other people. Any such device must be offered with a simultaneous willingness on our part to spend time listening and loving the one in need.

2. *Seek out someone* who's been through it before. Don't try to be a stiff-upper-lipped hero. Those who have been through death or divorce will be able to help you understand your feelings. If they have successfully resolved their grief and loneliness, they'll also provide a model of hope. Though everything that they did may not work for you, some of their suggestions will be of help. Just having someone to freely talk with is a tremendous source of strength.

3. *Keep stable the things that are stable* for a while. The grief process takes about two years to complete. If at all possible, try not to make major changes in your life situation during the first year after a death or divorce. Don't just up and sell your house, for example, because it has too many painful memories. Wait until you've worked through some of your grief and loneliness. You need points of familiarity and stability in what may seem like a raging sea of changes. As time goes on you may want to change the way your house is decorated, your job, or your place of residence. Some seem to need this, while others feel content keeping things the same. Do whatever feels best. But at first,

keep as much the same as you can. Listen to the Lord's quiet guidance, and don't get immersed in all the advice that will be showered on you at first. Everyone will try to help. As time goes on and you prayerfully formulate plans, seek feedback from friends who know you thoroughly.

4. One of the most effective ways to cope with the loneliness of loss is to *care for others*. Finding meaning by giving one's self to a person, idea, or cause greater than one's self has helped countless people handle their loneliness. We all need to be needed. When we reach out to help others, we establish a new link that gives us a sense of purpose and value. It can be as simple as feeding the neighbors' dog when they're on vacation, or volunteering in a hospital. Older people especially need to know they matter. Unless sickness intervenes, older widows and widowers can and do give of themselves consistently and significantly to others. For the Christian single (of any age), discovering and committing one's self wholeheartedly to fulfilling God's purpose in life is a highly significant key to living with a minimum of loneliness.

5. *Imagine yourself as not lonely*. Picture yourself making and enjoying new friendships. You've got to will to be different. Many older widows and widowers need to even will to live. Try to avoid Valium, alcohol, and other drugs which seem to interfere with the ability to visualize and creatively imagine yourself in new situations and relationships.

6. Make sure you get *regular exercise and good nutrition*. There is a tendency to let ourselves go when we've lost a partner. Because we are finely tuned systems, what we eat undoubtedly affects our emotions. Some initial loss of weight is common, but don't neglect proper eating habits. The truth of the matter is that someone needs to write a book — *Recipes for One* — to help single people adjust to the changes in buying and cooking food. Studies show that good nutrition and vigorous exercise help us to think more clearly, ventilate our emotions, and be less easily depressed.

7. *Learn life management skills*. This is especially important for older women who have not learned how to drive, who don't know how to make simple home repairs or how to handle finances. Without these skills the widow or divorcée finds herself feeling helpless. We've already seen the connection between helplessness, depression, and loneliness. Loneliness is intensified because she finds herself ready to turn to her husband, but he is not there. She has no one to turn to who cares, except the professionals, and they cost too much. Also, lack of such a basic skill as driving a car may physically isolate her from friends and intensify her loneliness. Learning basic skills gives her a feeling of competence and confidence that she can make it.

The same holds true for the widower or divorced male. Usually, learning how to cook is the most difficult thing, though taking care of children if there is no housekeeper can be a frightening task as well. You can learn these various skills at adult education classes or in special groups for widows, widowers, and the divorced. This is an area of ministry that churches could develop much more extensively in cooperation with funeral homes and divorce courts.

8. *Discover the worst time of day* for you, and change your schedule. In addition to holidays and special days, many people find that certain times of the day or days of the week are especially lonely. Many widows report that sundown is difficult. Or it may be a time that you and your spouse regularly did something together. Try to do something such as take your dog for a walk, or schedule a regular phone call to a friend. Don't sit around passively and pine away. Second, try to substitute a different activity if you and your spouse did something particular at that time.

9. Finally, *turn to God*. He understands. A number of studies show that bereaved people with well-defined church affiliations adjust better.[4] This is due to their private relationship with the Heavenly Father who understands death and grief. It's also due to the support of a closely knit community that has the ability to

surround and support the grieving person with prayer, affection, and practical help.

In sum, people who are fairly independent (don't feel help-less), have ongoing personal interests, are economically secure, have a satisfying commitment to God, are concerned for others, and have long-term friendships adjust best to the loss of a spouse through divorce or death.[5]

Before turning to retirement, I'd like to briefly suggest some ways to help children cope with their parents' divorce or death. It is only in this century that American children have been so shielded from death. Children are not allowed to experience the dying of a brother, sister, grandparents, or parent because death has been moved from the home to the hospital. Death intrudes into the child's awareness, regardless, when his pet kitty dies or he says, "Now I lay me down to sleep, I pray the Lord my soul to keep. If I should die before I wake...." At first children see death as a temporary departure. They've learned that Mommy and Daddy always come back. Preschoolers will find it difficult to understand permanent loss. They will sense that something wrong has happened due to the grieving of the remaining parent. As children get older, they begin to see death as a boogey man or some evil person.

It is probably best to talk about death as it happens naturally in a child's world. Conversation should focus on life but matter of factly convey that all life ends sometime. Allow the kids to freely ask questions, and try to answer simply and straight-forwardly. If a child loses a parent, *don't* tell him or her that God took his Daddy home to heaven. To a small child who loves his Daddy, anyone who takes Daddy away must be cruel. Rather, try to explain things in natural terms. Often children will simply accept the facts without asking the adult "Why?"

In cases of both death and divorce, children need special assurance that they're loved. In cases of divorce, children often assume that they are somehow to blame for Mommy and Daddy not living together. They may feel that the parent who has left doesn't love *them* because if somebody loves somebody they live with them. They must be reassured by both parents that each of the parents loves them and that the divorce has nothing to do with them. Try to work out regular visits with the departed parent that are not marked by conflict between adults; parents should avoid making cutting and angry comments about the former partner. At least for a while, it's probably best not to date if there are young children; this introduces confusion into the child's mind.

Retirement

At the turn of the century, average life expectancy was 47 years. Now it is 70.4 years. Over 10 percent of the American population is over 65; that amounts to more than 21 million people. More than 4,000 Americans retire each day. This portion of our population is growing faster than any other group. By the year 2000 there will probably be 33 million retirees.[6]

Retirement is a significant step in life because it signals a major change in how society views us. Our society places top value upon those who produce goods and services for the benefit of our economic system. Those who achieve the most are paid and honored the most. They're wooed and wanted. They belong. Upon retirement, we lose our ability to produce in ways society values. We're no longer sought out for advice or "friendship." We often discover that many of our so-called friendships were only due to the role we had at work. Our desk is taken away, our position redefined, and we may well find ourselves unwelcome at the place where we gave many of our best years. It's not that people are being mean. It's just that "business is business," and we no longer count. This realization plunges many men into depression and loneliness. (Though I suspect women will be feeling the impact of retirement more and more in years to come, the work world is still primarily for men.) Mandatory retirement is especially difficult to take because it says that overnight, when you turn the magic age, you're no longer capable.

Retirement may also further isolation because of tensions between husband and wife. If the wife has been used to "ruling the castle" during the work hours, the presence of her husband may cause serious conflicts. Not knowing what else to do, some husands literally trail their wives around the house, asking questions, changing things, or just sitting. This is unnerving, to say the least.

Finally, retirement may increase loneliness because of changed relationships with children. There may not be as much money to enable the retirees to get together with their children if a great distance separates them. Also, the parents' position may gradually become one of increasing dependency. This lack of independence may lead to lonely withdrawal by the parents and even rejection by children who don't want to assume responsibility.

Adjustment to the loneliness of depression can be helped in several ways:

1. Those who adjust best start preparing for retirement early. They make realistic plans. They develop hobbies they can afford and find interesting. They begin to spend more time on friendships and less on "success" in their later work years.

2. Many retirees find purpose and relief from loneliness by getting involved in some kind of part-time work. This may be the extension of a hobby such as woodworking, or it may be a new "career" such as in real estate, furniture repair, or various mail order businesses.

3. They work out an understanding with their wives, in advance, about around the house behaviors that are mutually acceptable. A smart wife will begin thinking of ways she can transfer some of her responsibility to her husband to keep him busy.

4. They become involved in helping other people. This can range from teaching various skills (carpentry, plumbing, etc.) to young boys to acting as consultants to colleges or other groups that could benefit from their expertise. Many retired businessmen keep active and satisfied doing this kind of work.

5. They may become *more* rather than less involved in church programs. There is no reason for a healthy retiree to fade into oblivion in the church. Teachers, janitors, bus drivers, and people to work on evangelism or various kinds of practical assistance are always needed. Retirees can also become vital leaders and participants in a prayer ministry. They can complement a pastor's ministry by doing one-on-one discipleship with new believers.

While the impact of loss through moving, death, divorce, and retirement can never be completely removed, the determined use of the practical guidelines given in this chapter will help lessen the feelings of loneliness that disrupted attachments always bring.

11
ULTIMATE INTIMACY

There are times when no one else can really understand how we feel, no one seems to care, or people seem too busy to meet our needs. Even the closest relationships have cycles of intimacy and distance. When we're lonely and there is no one to turn to, it's very easy to start blaming and to become disillusioned with people who aren't acting as we expect and need. We tend to place greater demands on them and usually end up even more isolated. Or, we may look further and further inward, drawing into a protective shell, refusing to expose ourselves any longer to other people who seem so insensitive to us.

Even if our relationships with others are generally satisfactory, there is a sense in which we always stand alone. We were born and we die in our own psychological space. There are the times also when we wonder what life is all about, who we are, why we exist. And there is the facing of death — no one can go through it with us, or replace a loved one who has died. For those without a sense of connection with ultimate meaning that transcends the daily routines of life, there is a deep sense of existential loneliness that other people can't totally remedy. Existentialist writers such as Sartre and Camus have written eloquently about the anguish, alienation, and loneliness that fill a life without God. Life without God is impersonal and irrational. There is no lasting intimacy because purpose often becomes self-centered, and people become merely a means to fill our inner needs.

At the deepest levels of our being, only God can satisfy us. *Ultimate intimacy depends upon finding, knowing, and sharing God.* We need each other dearly, but others can never be enough. As we establish and deepen our relationship with God, we'll experience an underlying sense of communion and acceptance that people and events can't destroy. Because God made us, He knows us thoroughly and does not abandon us.

O Lord, you have searched me and you know me. You know when I sit and when I rise; you perceive my thoughts from afar. You discern my going out and my lying down; you are familiar with all my ways. Before a word is on my tongue you know it completely, O Lord. You hem me in, behind and before; you have laid your hand upon me. Such knowledge is too wonderful for me, too lofty for me to attain. Where can I go from your Spirit? Where can I flee from your presence? If I go up to the heavens, you are there; if I make my bed in the depths, you are there. If I rise on the wings of the dawn, if I settle on the far side of the sea, even there your hand will guide me, your right hand will hold me fast.... For you created my inmost being; you knit me together in my mother's womb.... My frame was not hidden from you when I was made in the secret place. When I was woven together in the depths of the earth, your eyes saw my unformed body. All the days ordained for me were written in your book before one of them came to be.[1]

As we set our hearts on knowing and serving God, He allows us to enjoy an abiding depth of companionship that even the dearest spouse or friend can't provide (Proverbs 18:24b). He also grants us a basic sense of connection and purpose in life that helps us find meaning in life and lessens loneliness.

Finding God

It has been estimated that over 2 billion people in the world have definite religious commitments.[2] These include Buddhism,

Confucianism, Christianity, Islam, Judaism, Shintoism, and Taoism, among others. Some of these religions view God as an impersonal, pantheistic force with whom we ultimately merge by losing our identity. The meditation of Eastern religions is seen as a way of merging with the cosmos, becoming one, by emptying our minds of all rational thought. Loneliness is overcome as we lose ourselves in that which is beyond us, as we deny our personality and past, according to such approaches.

Not so with Christianity. According to the Old and New Testaments, God is Spirit, but He is not impersonal. He is a Person. He describes Himself in personal terms — "I am" (Exodus 3:13-14). Even the Holy Spirit is never referred to as "it." The act of incarnation that brought God to earth in visible form further confirmed His nature as a willing, thinking, feeling, acting Person. Because God is personal, it is possible to establish a close relationship with Him.

How can we do this? How can human beings establish an intimate relationship with God? It begins by accepting an invitation. God invites us to become His adopted children (John 1:12-13). He wishes to love and care for us as part of His family. Our second son is adopted. We wanted him very much and were delighted after a period of waiting and uncertainty to finally hold him in our arms. We did not want him, however, so that we could dominate him or make him feel inferior. Rather, we wanted him to love and to nurture into his full potential. At the same time he will always be our son, and hold a special place in our hearts, just like our two natural-born sons.

What is the invitation? God simply asks us to accept spiritual adoption. The process He has established is to accept the sacrifice of Jesus the God-Son as our Savior. Instead of dying as enemies of God, we can be "born" into His family. Instead of living a spiritually alienated life, we can experience intimacy with God Himself. This is because Jesus satisfied the need for justice. He was able to stand satisfactorily in our place because He was perfect. Jesus claimed to be the Messiah, God, incurring the wrath of religious leaders of His day (John 8:58-59). He also said He was *the* way, truth, and life; Jesus became the communication link between God and people (John 14:6); from the beginning He was the Word and remains so today. In addition, He performed numerous miracles witnessed by thousands. This is not the place to develop an apologetic supporting the divinity and claims of Jesus, however. Other books such as *Evidence That Demands a Verdict* (Josh McDowell) and *Mere Christianity* (C. S. Lewis) do so very clearly and completely.

The way to ultimate intimacy with God is accepting God's verdict of us as morally imperfect and sinful beings who naturally rebel against Him. By repenting, or turning our will against sin and toward God, we can turn our rebellion to communion. In God's eyes each sin is as heinous as murder is to us, because sin breaks the fellowship He intended us to have and disrupts the whole created order, tipping it into disorder, grief, evil, and alienation. Once we have admitted, repented, and received, God gives us the special gift of His Holy Spirit to live in us, to comfort and guide us. Instead of losing our identity in some undefined nothingness, we become new creatures with God's Spirit in us (2 Corinthians 5:17). We become part of the family of God.

The process of coming to God through Jesus differs from person to person. Some people do not remember the exact moment they made the decision to say yes to adoption. Many others experience a process of learning about Jesus through an acquaintance, friend, tract, radio program, or television show. They then go through some life crisis that brings them to a definite point of decision; they see their lives are a mess and that they need God. In the face of God's beckoning love they forsake being spiritually homeless orphans. They give up the freedom of spiritual independence and rebellion for the freedom of His love. Some argue that this is too exclusive. The process *is* definite, but it only excludes those who refuse to accept God's Truth and Way. God doesn't exclude; people rebel. Perhaps we can understand things better if we realize that there are definite legal rules and procedures for adoption. We can argue all we want, or try to adopt a child using our own rules, but that child is not part of the family until we've followed the process established by authorities. Until we follow the process God has set up, we won't belong to His family. The failure to follow is ours, not God's; He gives each of us multiple invitations.

Recently we did some research to see what difference being born again and having an inner commitment to God would make with regard to loneliness, purpose in life, and well-being.[3] Those who were born again were much more "intrinsic" in their religious commitment — their faith was not an abstract philosophy or ritual but an inner, pervasive part of them. We found that born-again Christians had significantly higher levels of both religious well-being (relationship with God) and existential well-being (life satisfaction and life purpose) than either "ethical" Christians, who try to follow the ethical and moral teachings of Christ without asking Christ into their lives as Savior and Lord, or non-Christians. People who were born again were more excited about life, had more purpose and meaning, saw their lives as more worthwhile, and felt more prepared for death. Born-again Christians were the least lonely. Non-Christians most frequently felt that they lacked companionship, were completely alone, were unable to reach out and communicate, and weren't close to anyone. They most frequently felt lonely.

Knowing God

Finding that God is not a cold abstraction or an impersonal force but our loving Heavenly Father is only the *beginning* of the relationship. As we get to know Him and open ourselves to His love, we are able to enter into a deeply satisfying companionship. We find that Jesus is unchanging. He isn't fickle; we can count on Him to be consistent. We learn that God is steadfast love (Psalm 136). He loved us first, He loves us in spite of our unloveliness, and He'll continue to love us as His children. This is because He *is* Love (as well as Justice). What more could we ask for than someone who cares deeply, understands us thoroughly, is completely trustworthy, and always acts on our behalf?

The problem is that it takes a while for us to really *believe* this. We may know about it and agree it is so, but we have to give God a chance to show us His loving character. Knowing God intimately is a process; it doesn't happen all at once. Building intimacy with God involves taking risks of faith that reveal His goodness, as well as passing tests of our own trustworthiness. God reveals Himself fully to those *He* can trust because their hearts are set on loving and following Him. Likewise, we become more and more willing to open ourselves to His ways as we see that risking brings an ever deeper sense of communion between Him and us. This is not to say that there are always immediate rewards — some people feel that God is with them *because* they got the house they wanted, the job they longed for, the promotion they desired. Many fail to realize that God is just as much with them when following Him brings misunderstanding and persecution. If we persist in believing even when outward signs stir mistrust, God will reward us days or months later with a special experience of His grace.

There are a number of principles and practices that are given to God's children to meet their basic spiritual need, which is simply knowing God's love in personal experience. As we bask in God's love and companionship, our loneliness is greatly lessened. It will probably not be removed if we only follow the first part of the great commandment — "Love the Lord your God with all your heart and with all your soul and with all your strength and with all your mind" — but it surely will if we also "Love your neighbor as yourself" (Luke 10:27). But more about that later. Right now the question is, How can we know God more fully and experience a close relationship with Him?

First, God has given us His Spirit to live in us when we become His children. He does not obliterate our identity but purifies it. The importance of this gift is seen in Romans 8:26-27, where we're told that God's Spirit knows and communicates God's thoughts to us. He also ''helps us in our weakness'' and intercedes for us in divine language, language unrestricted by words. The Spirit draws God and man together. This is why we're commanded to be filled with the Spirit (Ephesians 5:18) and warned not to grieve Him (Ephesians 4:30). The Spirit is hindered in mediating for us when we grieve Him through willful or unconfessed sin. We become isolated from God until things are straightened out in a biblical manner. Interestingly, many of the sins which grieve God's Spirit also separate us from others. These include lying, anger, stealing, unwholesome talk, bitterness, rage, malice, brawling, and slander (Ephesians 4:25-31). That is why confession of sins is not only a private matter with God (1 John 1:9) but must involve setting things right with others (Matthew 5:23-24). If we sin privately against God, it's between us and Him; if others are involved, confession must include those specific people. Confession restores relationships because it removes defensiveness and hostility. When we ask forgiveness we make peace, because we admit our wrongs and focus on healing rather than on rights. Confession allows us to be vulnerable and intimate because we're not hiding behind pride or blame. By following this guideline we free the Spirit to fill us. As the Spirit is allowed to fully live in us, we experience an ever deepening love and companionship both with God and with others.

Knowing God extends beyond knowledge *about* God. It requires more than simple agreement to a creed or statement, as we've seen in the responsibility we have for confession. This is an important point, because in many Christian circles today we seem to have substituted easy-belief for a walk with God that affects our whole life. We can easily think that simply *saying* the right things is enough. It isn't. God requires faith that engages our whole being. Knowing God requires *wholeheartedness* (Proverbs 2:1-5). It must be a top priority, not an option, if we are to fully enjoy God. Knowing God is not a benefit for the casual Christian. Casual commitment produces superficial acquaintance with God, not the joy of intimacy. Knowing God is not the result of detached, objective study. We can study God theologically until we're blue in the face and still not really know Him personally. Knowing God is involved knowing. It requires us to give ourselves. We must *behave* our faith as well as believe. God reveals Himself to us as He sees our love toward Him through our obedience. Jesus made it clear, "If you love me, you will obey what I command" (John 14:15). James affirmed that "a person is justified by what he does and not by faith alone" (James 2:24). The test of our faith comes in the decisions we make. It is then that our true priorities are most clearly revealed.[4] We will find that God reveals Himself to us as we follow His guidelines for living. These extend into every area of life, including ethics in business. If we fail to take this principle of behaving belief seriously, we basically question the integrity of God and will never experience a close walk with Him.

God has also given us the miracle of *prayer*. Prayer is more than asking for things in a pinch. It's not autohypnosis in any normal sense because prayers are answered quite apart from any subsequent presence or influence of ours. It is more than just a prescribed ritual with holy-sounding intonations. It is our private communication system with God. Prayer is our opportunity to openly and honestly discuss the deepest longings and most distressing needs of our hearts with our loving and accepting Heavenly Father. We don't need to hold back for fear of rejection. In 1 Peter 5:7 we're encouraged to "Cast all [our] anxiety upon him because he cares for [us]." We're encouraged to ask God for specific help (Matthew 7:7-11) and are given the promise that as we do this with thanksgiving we will experience His peace (Philippians 4:7). We can ask Him to give practical insights, patience, the ability to adjust our expectations, a special indwelling of His Spirit that will fill our emptiness, to change pessimistic thinking and give us hope, to bring us into satisfying new friendships, to fill our life with His purposes, and to give us new experiences of His love.

Of vital importance is the fact that prayer is intended to be a two-way system. Prayer is not just pious monologue. It is not just a way to ask for things, though we're encouraged to do that. Prayer at its best is *dialogue*; we listen and we speak. Most of us are too busy asking and entertaining God with praise to listen. But it's in two-way prayer that we really connect with God. In two-way prayer God quietly and lovingly responds through His Spirit. He comforts, gives insight, brings us renewed strength, and speaks hope. Most of us are too impatient to wait. And yet, if dialogue is one of our deep human needs, and the absence of dialogue fosters loneliness, we need to start listening. But dialogue is also made up of genuine expression. Many Christians are limited to restricted forms of praying which don't express their needs. When we don't tell God the way things *really* are, we shortchange Him and shortchange ourselves. Prayer becomes boring unless it contains the substance of real-life concerns. When we're not honest with God, we also tend to start talking to others about things better kept quiet, seeking sympathy and advice by hashing out our problems over and over with nothing much changing. God stands poised, ready to hear what's really on our minds and able to give by His Spirit the subtle impulses that provide new perspectives and solutions.

Prayer needs to happen regularly. It can be an ongoing conversation throughout the day, but there are also times when we need to sit down and have good long talks with Him, as we would with any close companion. These need to be unhurried times when we can talk out our concerns and spend adequate time listening. Many of God's greatest saints have regularly spent three or four hours a day in this kind of prayer — worshiping, petitioning, praising, and knowing God.

The practice of prayer together with others also provides a special kind of intimacy between partners. As the needs of others and ourselves are brought jointly to the Father, and our hearts are lifted in petition and praise, we will find that warm, close bonds develop with others who express their dependency upon our Father along with us. As we commune together with our Father, we will find it easier to commune with each other. This is especially true when prayer groups are fairly small and genuine needs are expressed.

Worship is another vital part of knowing God. Worship is more than a ritual. In worship we join together with others to jointly celebrate the wonderful love and character of God our Father and Jesus our Savior. Worship brings us close to God because it is a time of intentionally drawing near to Him in appreciation. It is a time of giving rather than a time of receiving. As we give our gratitude and praise we will receive, but that should not be our primary intent. Our purpose is to honor God with our expressions of His faithfulness. True worship involves both our mind and emotions. It is much more than an informationally oriented sermon or an exhilarating emotional experience. Worship that is *only* mentally oriented eventually leaves us feeling dry inside, wishing for a deeper experience of God's personal presence. There is a place for sound biblical and doctrinal instruction, as well as evangelistic messages, but these should not be confused with worship. Worship that centers *only* on emotional exhilaration eventually leaves us feeling abandoned by God. Worship that requires a continual "high" will only bring us low. God more often reveals Himself deeply to us in the quiet moments of our daily life than in moments of exhilaration. Worship that knits our affections to God recounts the times and ways in which God has met the needs of His people. More specifically, it provides definite opportunities for us to privately and publicly recount the ways that He has met our needs. True worship also includes specific expressions of thanksgiving as well as forgiveness of specific, confessed sin. As we are given opportunity to sing, meditate, and express our gratitude, we are flooded with love for our Savior. The public nature of worship provides opportunity to lift each other up through shared gratitude.

Often it seems that music and testimony are seen as preludes to "worship," which is viewed as the sermon. In truth, these are central to the lifting of our affections toward God. All too often we seem to be more locked into a proper execution of four-part harmony, requiring careful attention to prescribed notes in our hymnals, than we are into really expressing our love to God. Music that frees us to worship focuses our attention and feelings on the Savior rather than on performance or performers. Perhaps we should do away with hymnals, memorize hymns, and not worry about perfect harmony when we sing! The use of simple choruses is a help, though choruses shouldn't replace the great hymns of our faith. Testimony includes both God's work in our personal lives, and listening to what God is doing in other places and lives. Missions reports are vital to worship. Regular input about what God's Spirit is specifically doing throughout the world helps us to keep trusting Him when things seem to be rather routine in our own neck of the woods.

Although I have emphasized group worship in the community of believers, I want to hasten to add that worship should be a part of personal "devotions" and can be part of the spiritual communion of husbands and wives.

The ingredients of true worship, then, are remembering the works of God toward His people, recounting His character, and expressing gratitude for specific ways He has forgiven our sins and met our needs. Music and public testimony should be designed to help us lift our spirits in communion beyond what a private and highly intellectualized (by this I mean emotionally detached) approach will do.

Our worship experience is also deepened as we allow ourselves to enter the *fellowship of faith*. This is simply being willing to follow God's leading when risks are involved. There is a kind of Christianity that puts security first and faith second. If we shirk from following God into the hard spots, we will never experience the depth of His trustworthy love. It's as we experience His faithfulness in response to our obedience that we come to know more fully the wonder of His gentle, personal care. For some, the fellowship of faith may even lead to suffering. Biblically, suffering provides the believer with a chance to thoroughly identify with the suffering Savior. It is a chance to experience the greatness of His love and the comforting His Spirit provides. This doesn't mean that we are to look for suffering; if we're normal we don't. But if we should suffer for His sake, we will know God more intimately than we ever could otherwise.

Finally, God has exhorted us to *memorize and meditate on His Word*. In Joshua 1:8-9 we read, ''Do not let this Book of the Law depart from your mouth; meditate on it day and night, so that you may be careful to do everything written in it. Then you will be prosperous and successful. Have I not commanded you? Be strong and courageous. Do not be terrified; do not be discouraged, for the Lord your God will be with you wherever you go.'' As we make God's thoughts part of us, we become better able to keep His perspective on the situations we find ourselves in. As we become immersed in the Scripture, we not only draw closer to God, but we also find specific helps and promises for our situations and needs. For example, the Psalms are full of the expressions of David's loneliness, his cries to God, His recounting of God's faithfulness and steadfast love, and hope in the midst of intense need. Other Scriptures give us promises of answers to prayer, the comforting of God's Spirit, and the clear sense that the pain we may have to endure now is not the end of the story! I have included a number of verses that should prove helpful in times of loneliness in Table 11.1. If these and other passages are memorized and meditated upon, they will help us build positive thought structures and a spiritual-emotional reservoir that will help us cope in times of loneliness. The time to memorize is *before* we are plunged into loneliness, because when we're feeling intensely lonely, it's difficult to summon the emotional reserves and concentration necessary to do much more than read or pray the verses (which is also an important use of Scripture).

Table 11.1

SCRIPTURAL AIDS TO OVERCOMING LONELINESS

Prayer Psalms and Promises

Psalm 16: 7-11
Psalm 18: 1-6, 27-29
Psalm 25: 16-18
Psalm 27: 7-10
Psalm 34: 1-6, 17-18
Psalm 40: 1-4
Psalm 42: 5-11
Psalm 69
Psalm 71
Psalm 73: 25-28
Psalm 77: 1-15
Psalm 86: 1-13
Psalm 119: 25-32, 49-52,
    73-80, 89-93
Psalm 142
Psalm 143: 5-8
Luke 11: 9-13
James 1: 5-6

God is Our Refuge and Deliverer

Psalm 18: 24
Psalm 23
Psalm 36: 5-9

Psalm 37: 23-24
Psalm 46: 1
Psalm 61: 1-4
Psalm 68: 19-20
John 14: 16-23
1 Peter 5: 6-9

The Hope of God's Character and Faithfulness

Psalm 66
Psalm 84
Psalm 95
Psalm 103
Psalm 104
Psalm 107: 1-9
Psalm 116
Psalm 145
Psalm 146
Psalm 147: 1, 3, 5

Knowing God

Isaiah 59: 1-2
Romans 10: 9-13
Ephesians 2: 8-10
1 John 1: 5-10
1 John 5: 1-4

Endurance

Romans 5: 1-5
Hebrews 12: 1-2
James 1: 2-4
1 Peter 1: 6-9

God's Understanding

Psalm 139: 1-18, 23-24
Isaiah 53: 3-4

The Healing Power of God

Matthew 8: 3
Matthew 8: 27
Matthew 9: 6-8
Matthew 9: 35-36
Mark 5: 34, 39-43
Mark 6: 41-42
Mark 7: 37
Luke 18: 42-43
John 11: 43-44

Healing Community

John 13: 34-35
John 15: 12

Romans 12: 10-18
Romans 14: 19
Romans 15: 7
Galatians 6: 2
Ephesians 4: 1-3
Philippians 2: 1-8
Colossians 3: 12-16
1 John 4: 7

Constructive Thinking/Peace

Romans 12: 2
Ephesians 4: 17-20
Philippians 4: 6-9
Colossians 2: 8
1 Thessalonians 5: 16-18

Purpose in Life

Isaiah 58: 6-12
Matthew 28: 19-20
Acts 1: 8
Romans 12: 1
Ephesians 1: 3-12
Philippians 3: 7-16

Sharing God and Witnessing for Him

Knowing God also involves witnessing for Him. When we tell others about Jesus, we automatically reflect on who He is and what He has done for us. As we witness we affirm our relationship with Him. There is probably no greater joy than seeing someone experience the miracle of spiritual regeneration as a result of our witness. There is a special bond between the two people, and a special love for Jesus that results from effective witnessing. On both levels we experience a sense of joyous intimacy. When the person who comes to know Jesus as Savior is someone that we have known and specifically prayed for, there is a tender sense of affection such as caused Paul to comment, "We loved you so much that we were delighted to share with you not only the gospel of God but our lives as well, because you had become so dear to us" (1 Thessalonians 2:8).

We share God when we love one another in practical ways. The Scripture plainly states: "This is how we know what love is: Jesus Christ laid down his life for us. And we ought to lay down our lives for our brothers. If anyone has material possessions and sees his brother in need but has no pity on him, how can the love of God be in him? Dear children, let us not love with words or tongue but with actions and in truth" (1 John 3:16-18). Paul also emphasizes that "If you have any encouragement from being united with Christ, if any comfort from his love, if any fellowship with the Spirit, if any tenderness and compassion, then make my joy complete by being like-minded, having the same love, being one in spirit and purpose" (Philippians 2:1-2).

Because God made us as social beings, ultimate intimacy comes when we love God *and* love others wholeheartedly. We are drawn together and to God as we incarnate the love of Jesus in our relationships. The community of believers is central throughout Scripture. Being the people of God is never a matter of individualism. Knowing God takes place most often in the context of community in both the Old and New Testaments. Sharing God means to let His Spirit dominate in our relationships. It is then that we are able to "clothe [our]selves with compassion, kindness, humility, gentleness and patience" (Colossians 3:12). Christian community is to be a place of acceptance, forgiveness, and forbearance; it is not to be a place of comparison and competition. As the people of God work to put Christ's love into practice between themselves, loneliness disappears. The true indication of a church's spiritual stature is not how many people attend but how thoroughly its people love and are loved by one another. I want to emphasize that this love is not just a feeling of togetherness when we're in a church service. It is a practical love that senses and satisfies the needs of one another.

As we close this book, I'd like to briefly suggest some ways that Christian churches can be communities rather than institutions, ways that it can help more people toward ultimate intimacy:

1. *Counter societal values which promote loneliness.* We have seen that key societal values of autonomy, achievement, acquisition, appearance, and actualization promote loneliness. The church must carefully avoid the intrusion of these values as central determinants of our choices and relationships. If we allow them to guide us, several things which increase loneliness will happen. First, with success as our banner we will focus on institutional development. People will be seen more as means for evaluating success than as those to be ministered to; we will emphasize the size of our institution more than the quality of our community. Second, those who don't appear to be "good fits" in our formula of success are likely to be avoided. These most likely will include physically or mentally handicapped people, racial minorities, the elderly, the poor and unemployed, and immigrants, among others. In the process we will only intensify the feelings of rejection and isolation of those who aren't "good enough" and establish "performance" as the basis of acceptance. Third, once we have established performance as our foundation, we make it less likely that people can be genuine about their needs, because to reveal weaknesses will be seen as an indication of failure. We end up playing the "Sunday" game in which everyone presents himself as okay; but in truth many are deeply hurting and need freedom to be honest.

We must counter these values by emphasizing that the church is first of all a place of community and communion. The basis of acceptance is to be loved, not power. The church must be a place where people can belong because of Christ's love, not because of human performance. We must be careful not to slip into institutional success thinking. Preachers must challenge secular values and give guidance on alternative ways to orient our lives. Sunday school and small groups should periodically focus on ways to live against the value system which promotes self-centeredness and separation. Some churches seem to have substituted psychology for the Word of God, for example. Their emphasis is almost exclusively on personal happiness and self-fulfillment rather than on holiness and servanthood. We need to be careful to strike a balance between practical and personal preaching, on the one hand, and a doctrinal orientation which ignores people in the quest for theological perfection on the other. There are those in our churches who have deep needs and need professional psychological counseling. All of us need to have sermons which connect to our daily lives. But sermons must first point us to the Savior and not to ourselves. The source of our strength and hope is in God's love and responsiveness, not in knowing ourselves. If we are encouraged to only turn inward, we are likely to lose the very perspective which helps overcome loneliness — the giving of ourselves to love God and serve Him, which in part involves loving others. Happiness is the by-product of our walk with God, not the aim.

2. *Be a healing community.* Although preaching and Bible study need to be God-centered, the church must also encourage practical and healing love. For those with problems, including loneliness, there needs to be understanding, emotional support, and professional help rather than condemnation and detached, moralistic pronouncements. Truth must be wrapped in grace. For all of us, there need to be structures and opportunities for revealing and meeting needs. Ritual and tradition must be adapted to address the needs of people.

With regard to the lonely, there are several practical ways in which this may be done. For example, a *needs and helps exchange* might be developed so that older people, widows, and the divorced, as well as others, can have practical needs known and met. In one church, for example, the men got together and completely reroofed the house of a young divorced woman. A variation of this is to develop *matches.* In one church, the young people are each matched with senior citizens and regularly visit, call, and do practical chores like painting and yardwork. Because of the increase in divorces, matches need to be encouraged between men in the church and young boys living with their mothers; the same can be done between women and girls. A regular babysitting service might also be offered to single parents at low or no cost to allow them needed time for activities without the children. Retirees also might be able to teach a variety of skills and enjoyable hobbies to children and teens.

Another way in which needs for companionship can be helped is through the development of *church-sponsored apartment buildings*. This has been done by a number of churches for elderly citizens, but the time has come to build so that divorced parents and their children can also be included. This would allow for the development of ''extended families'' from a church or churches. In this kind of setting, with proper architectural and community planning, the residents will be able to care for each other more than in the normal fleeting Sunday contacts. *Extended families* should be encouraged for those not living in such buildings as well. Intergenerational Sunday school classes can bring children, teens, young, middle, and older adults together in meaningful study and activity.[5] One of the most delightful experiences that my family has had in our past two churches is the love of adopted ''grandparents'' and ''aunts and uncles.'' Because we are geographically separated from our natural families, we have felt it important for our children to have more regular contact with an extended family. So we've ''adopted'' and been adopted by people in the past two churches who have loved the children like their own. I'll never forget my middle son's comment when he jumped up and down after we were going to visit Marc and Vernice — ''We're going to Grandma and Grandpa's.'' It dawned on me that they, Harold and Jean, and Helen really have been Grandpa and Grandma to the kids, as have their natural grandparents. In the process of sharing meals, outings, games, and special days with these and other dear ones, we've come to love and be loved in ways otherwise not possible. I've heard that some churches are creating households for extended families with singles and widowed persons moving into designated homes with an intact family. There are a number of hesitations that I have about this variation, but I'm sure that this and other types of communal, extended family arrangements will increase in the years ahead as Christians try to find places of day-to-day belonging.

Small group opportunities are also vitally important for those who are lonely. In these groups people can more easily reveal needs and receive focused love and help than in larger services. These groups may take the form of more traditional Bible study groups, focus on topics, or be developed around age groups. Churches should consider periodically sponsoring study groups on specific life needs and transitions in addition to inductive or topical Bible study (for example — "How to raise children as a single parent"; "Growing old joyfully"). These groups would tend to be more experientially-oriented and allow for personal disclosure, but they should also be grounded in the Word or they become airing sessions without much direction or helpful guidance.

Another possibility is to form *special interest groups*. Often people in churches don't know one another outside of superficial Sunday contacts. Interest groups may be formed around hobbies (for example — coin collecting, quilting, model railroading, ceramics), recreational interests, professions, or common life situations. The church must begin seeing itself as responsible for providing and promoting such informal coming together and communion.

Informal potlucks held weekly or so, combined with one of the above small-group formats, are often helpful for singles. Only those providing food for a specific meal are obligated to come, but all are welcome. Such informal, regular times provide a sense of belonging without the burden of formal commitment.

Those who have been through loneliness episodes need to be encouraged to reach out to those suffering in similar situations. Just having someone we can freely talk and anguish with without fear and with a sense of being understood is a tremendous source of strength. This is an excellent ministry for those who have resolved their singleness or have satisfactorily worked through death or divorce. Such people are able to help in ways no one else can. Pastors need to consider having a roster of such people, including them as part of the pastoral team when trying to minister to the grieving lonely, especially. We need to be regularly encouraged to reach out informally as well.

3. *Be sensitive to those who are prone to loneliness.* Specific church structures can be established to reach out to those in the church body who are likely to be experiencing loneliness. For example, churches need to be alert to those visiting who have just moved into the area. Visitor's cards should reveal this information. Because the first year after a move is typically a time of loneliness and desire to belong, community hospitality hosts and hostesses should be appointed. These may be according to geographical areas or life-situation (widows, young intact families, singles). The hosts should be prepared to invite newly moved people to their homes for occasional meals and to be alert to practical ways to help ease the transition.

Churches may also *select loneliness-prone groups* to shape special outreaches toward. These might be new immigrants, the handicapped, the recently widowed or divorced, and orphans or children of newly divorced, among others. The particular form of outreach will vary, of course. The key is to provide a community where these people will feel wanted, and assistance to help them adjust. New immigrants, for example, will need language training and help in getting settled, including a place to live and a job. Outreach to the handicapped might involve regular visits to their institutions for music, recreation, and tutoring. The newly widowed might be helped with estate arrangements, resettling, and other practical needs.

4. *Build self-esteem biblically.* For those who are lonely because they have difficulty accepting themselves and consequently are plagued by shyness or inability to give and accept

love, the church needs to help build positive self-worth. The root of the problem of low self-esteem is negative evaluation. Either others that are important to them give them feedback that they don't have what it takes on certain valued characteristics, or they compare themselves on those dimensions with others and come to the conclusion that they're inferior.

The Bible provides several important insights for building positive self-esteem. Those with extremely severe inferiority feelings may need intensive counseling in an atmosphere of acceptance in addition to these perspectives. First, the experience of God's love lifts our self-worth to new heights. The fact that He *chooses* us to be His children, dependent *only* upon our consent and not on our capacities, provides us with a new measure of worth. Though He knows us intimately, including the things that we try to hide even from ourselves, God loves us and accepts us. The fact that His love is a gift of grace and not something we must achieve removes the possibility that we aren't good enough. It also frees us from self-condemnation. For many people, the flooding of God's love as they trust Him and become new creatures (2 Corinthians 5:17) allows them to really accept themselves for the first time.

Secondly, the biblical focus is on *faithfulness*, not comparison with others. God commends us for being trustworthy and living as He expects, to the limits of our capacity. Each person is looked at individually (Romans 12:3) and has individual worth. As we grow in our ability to focus on God's standards of value, human norms and approval become less crucial to us. This is not to say that we can completely avoid comparison or not need affirmation — we can't and we do. The Bible recognizes this when it exhorts us to avoid being judgmental (critical without compassion) and to be forgiving and patient with each other (Colossians 3:12-14; Ephesians 4:1-3). Biblical community is to be a place of love and acceptance. God has also provided for those times when we fail to meet His standards by reminding us that He knows us and is ready to forgive our guilt immediately upon confession (1 John 1:9).

The *biblical emphasis on gifts* also elevates the importance of each person. It is clear that God has given each Christian gifts, and that every gift (hence, every person) is important (Romans 12:4-10; 1 Corinthians 12:4-27) to the Body of Christ! When we focus on one or a few of the gifts as more important, or fail to value everyone as Scripture indicates we should, we foster inferiority and isolation in at least some members of the Body. We need to work hard to identify and appreciate everyone's gifts, to include them and to benefit from their presence in the community. To the extent that we rely on "professionals" to run the church, we lose an excellent opportunity to build self-worth and a sense of belonging on the part of many "ordinary" people in the pews. Perhaps we also need to practice out-loud thanksgiving more regularly in our churches. This can be done through encouragement or appreciation cards placed in the pews for members to send notes on to each other, and by special occasions honoring those who are less visible than those who are always in the limelight.

5. *Provide professional counseling and referrals*. For those who are so intensely lonely and depressed that they are apparently unhelped by solid Bible teaching and a generally caring community, our churches need to be prepared to provide more-systematic, focused, and intensive counseling. Many churches are beginning church-related counseling centers, and the growth of evangelicals in psychologically related fields has increased dramatically in recent years. For example, there are about 1300 members of the Christian Association for Psychological Studies, and another 1300 members of the National Association of Christians for Social Work. Many of these people are licensed counselors. In addition, there are probably another 1500-2000 professionally trained evangelical psychologists, counselors, and social workers who don't belong to these groups.

6. *Accentuate the hope that knowing Jesus gives*. In an age of depression and despair, the church needs to emphasize the fact that God is "the Blessed Controller of all things" (1 Timothy 6:15, RSV), that what is will not always be, and that God knows us and cares about us. As we help each other experience the hope of an eternity bathed in God's love (Titus 3:7), we will look forward in optimism rather than in despair.

7. *Emphasize finding and following God's purpose for each person*. As we look around we readily discover people who have suffered devastating losses, have never married, or have had very unhealthy upbringings but are not overcome by depression and loneliness. They seem to have risen above their circumstances and to be able to bring inspiration and hope to others. They may be fairly well known — such as Corrie Ten Boom and Mother Teresa — or known only to a few. They are not plastic or unreal — they too have experienced moments of great loneliness and despair. But they share the experience of ultimate purpose as they have become immersed and enveloped in God's specific purposes for them. They have moved beyond themselves and found joy to be their companion rather than loneliness.

God has made each of us to carry out His purpose in a unique way. No one else has the same heredity, environmental experiences, location, history, and specific role that God has determined in His eternal plan. As churches help people understand their gifts and connect with the deep purposes of God for them, loneliness will be swallowed up in a life of giving and loving. Emptiness will be filled with meaning.

Notes

Chapter 1

1. M. B. Parlee, "The Friendship Bond," *Psychology Today* (October 1979): 43-54, 113-14.
2. H. Lopata, "Loneliness: Forms and Components," *Social Problems* 17 (1969): 248-61. Author is at the University of Chicago.
3. C. Rubinstein, P. Shaver, and L. A. Peplau, "Loneliness," *Human Nature* (February 1979): 58-65.
4. T. Brennan, "Some Social and Psychological Correlates of Adolescent Loneliness" (paper presented at the UCLA Research Conference on Loneliness, Los Angeles, May 1979). Author is at the Behavioral Research Institute, Boulder, Colorado.
5. D. Perlman, A. C. Gerson, and B. Spinner, "Loneliness Among Senior Citizens: An Empirical Report," *Essence* 2 (1978): 239-48.
6. S. Gordon, *Lonely in America* (New York: Simon & Schuster, 1976).
7. R. Weiss, *Loneliness: Emotional and Social Isolation* (Cambridge, Mass.: M.I.T., 1973).

Chapter 2

1. C. A. Krause, *Guyana Massacre* (New York: Berkeley, 1978).
2. "Behind the Cult Craze," *U.S. News & World Report* (Dec. 4, 1978).
3. D. Perlman and L. A. Peplau, "Toward a Social Psychology of Loneliness," in R. Gilmour and S. Duck, eds., *Personal Relationships in Disorder* (to be published by Academic Press).
4. G. L. Klerman, "The Age of Melancholy," *Psychology Today* (April 1979): 36-42, 88.
5. M. E. P. Seligman, *Helplessness* (San Francisco: Freeman, 1975).
6. M. Slade, "Depressed? Try Friends," *Psychology Today* (October 1978): 19.
7. J. Sangster and C. W. Ellison, "Mental Illness, Loneliness, and Helplessness," to be published in *Mental Health and Society*.
8. R. Schulz, "Effects of Control and Predictability on the Physical and Psychological Well-Being of the Institutionalized Aged," *Journal of Personality and Social Psychology* 33 (1976): 563-73.

9. J. Turnstall, *Old and Alone* (New York: Humanities, 1967).

10. R. Abrahams, "Mutual Help for the Widowed," *Social Work* 17:5 (1972): 54-61.

11. C. T. Hill, Z. Rubin, and L. A. Peplau, "Breakups Before Marriage: The End of 103 Affairs," *Journal of Social Issues* 32:1 (1976): 147-68.

12. M. Bragg, "A Comparison of Nondepressed and Depressed Loneliness" (paper presented at the UCLA Research Conference on Loneliness, Los Angeles, May 1979). Author is at the University of Illinois.

13. J. J. Lynch, *The Broken Heart: The Medical Consequences of Loneliness* (New York: Basic, 1977). All information regarding loneliness and premature death is taken from this book.

14. C. Parkes, *Bereavement: Studies of Grief in Adult Life* (New York: Inter. U. Pr., 1972).

15. M. Young, B. Benjamin, and C. Wallis, "Mortality of Widowers," *Lancet* 2 (1963): 454.

16. J. Hartog, "Loneliness and Drug Abuse: Some Speculations" (paper presented at the UCLA Research Conference on Loneliness, Los Angeles, May 1979). Author is at the University of California Medical Center, San Francisco.

17. *Human Behavior* (December 1978): 13.

18. T. Brennan, "Some Social and Psychological Correlates of Adolescent Loneliness."

19. W. H. Jones, "The Persistence of Loneliness," (part of *Toward a Psychology of Loneliness*, a symposium presented at the American Psychological Association, Toronto, August 1978). Author is at the University of Tulsa, Oklahoma.

20. D. Perlman, A. C. Gerson, and B. Spinner, "Loneliness Among Senior Citizens," pp. 239-48.

21. V. Sermat, "Satisfaction in Different Types of Interpersonal Relationships, Willingness to Take Social Risks, and Loneliness" (paper presented at the UCLA Research Conference on Loneliness, Los Angeles, May 1979). Author is at York University, Toronto.

22. C. W. Ellison and R. F. Paloutzian, "Assessing Quality of Life: Spiritual Well-Being and Loneliness" (paper presented at the American Psychological Association, Toronto, August 1978).

Chapter 3

1. All Scripture quotations are from the *New International Version* (Grand Rapids: Zondervan, 1978).

2. J. L. Johnson, *Loneliness Is Not Forever* (Chicago: Moody, 1979), pp. 93-94.

3. An excellent book giving a more detailed analysis of doubts is Os Guinness, *In Two Minds* (Downers Grove, Ill.: InterVarsity, 1976).

Chapter 4

1. G. Gerbner and L. Gross, "The Scary World of TV's Heavy Viewer," *Psychology Today* (April 1976): 41-45.

2. E. E. Ford and R. L. Zorn, *Why Be Lonely?* (Niles, Ill.: Argus, 1975).

3. A. A. Berger, "Fear of Feeling: Vicious Cycles in Videoland and the Real World," *Human Behavior* (May 1977): 73.
4. *Institute for Christian Resources, Inc., Newsletter*, San Jose, Cal. (Fall 1978).
5. J. J. Lynch, *The Broken Heart: The Medical Consequences of Loneliness*, p. 204.
6. J. B. Calhoun, "Population Density and Social Pathology," *Scientific American* 206 (1962): 139-48.
7. D. Appleyard and M. Lintell, "The Environmental Quality of City Streets: The Residents' Viewpoint," *Journal of the American Institute of Planners* 38 (1972): 84-101.
8. J. E. Singer, "Social and Psychological Impact of Transportation Noise" (paper presented at the Acoustical Society of America meeting, Washington, D.C., 1977).
9. See K. R. Schneider, *On the Nature of Cities* (San Francisco: Jossey-Bass, 1979) for a detailed and enlightening examination of the impact of the automobile, industrialization, zoning, and suburbanization on individual and societal quality of life in urban America.

Chapter 5
1. B. Wilson, "Is Loneliness Necesary?," *Contempo* (March 1977): 29.
2. M. H. Klaus and J. H. Kennell, *Maternal-Infant Bonding* (St. Louis: Mosby, 1976).
3. Appreciation is expressed to Mary Thiessen of World Impact, Los Angeles, for letting me tell this painful but true story.
4. C. H. Kempe, "Child Abuse and Neglect," in N. B. Talbot, ed., *Raising Children in Modern America* (Boston: Little, Brown, 1976), pp. 173-88.
5. M. Perlberg, "A New Mirror for Narcissus," *Human Behavior* (February 1977): 16-22.
6. L. Wolfe, "Why Some People Can't Love — An Interview with Otto Kernberg," *Psychology Today* (June 1978): 55-59.
7. R. A. Spitz, "Hospitalism: An Inquiry into the Genesis of Psychiatric Conditions in Early Childhood (A follow-up report)," *Psychoanalytic Study of the Child* 1 (1945): 53-74.
8. R. S. Illingsworth, "Crying in Infants and Children," *British Medical Journal* 1 (1955): 75-78.
9. J. Bowlby, *Separation: Anxiety and Anger*, Attachment and Loss, vol. 2 (New York: Basic, 1973), pp. 227-28.

Chapter 6
1. I. J. Tanner, *Loneliness: The Fear of Love* (New York: Harper & Row, 1973), p. 52.
2. L. McBurnery, *Every Pastor Needs a Pastor* (Waco, Tex.: Word, 1977), p. 64.
3. "The Miracle of Kübler-Ross," *Human Behavior* (September 1977).
4. P. G. Zimbardo, *Shyness: What It Is and What to Do about It* (Menlo Park, Cal.: Addison-Wesley, 1977), pp. 13-14. Most of the discussion on shyness is based on this book.
5. H. N. Wright, *Communication: Key to Your Marriage* (Glendale, Cal.: Regal, 1974), p. 54.

NOTES

239

Chapter 7

1. S. Provence and R. C. Lipton, *Infants in Institutions* (New York: Inter. U. Pr., 1963).
2. J. Bowlby, *Separation: Anxiety and Anger*.
3. J. J. Lynch, *The Broken Heart: The Medical Consequences of Loneliness*.
4. A. Nicholi, "The Fractured Family: Following It Into the Future," *Christianity Today* (May 25, 1979): 11-14.
5. C. Longfellow, "Divorce in Context: Its Impact on Children," in G. Levinger and O. C. Moles, eds., *Divorce and Separation: Context, Causes, and Consequences* (New York: Basic, 1979).
6. P. Shaver and C. M. Rubinstein, "The Effects of Parental Attachment and Loss During Childhood on Subsequent Adult Loneliness, Self-Esteem, and Health" (paper presented at the UCLA Research Conference on Loneliness, Los Angeles, May 1979). The senior author is at New York University. The information that follows regarding death, divorce, and loneliness is based on their study of over 20,000 adults.
7. Ibid.
8. P. Leiderman and G. Leiderman, "Affective and Cognitive Consequences of Polymatric Infant Care in the East African Highlands," in vol. 8 of A. Pick, ed., *Minnesota Symposium on Child Development* (Minneapolis: U. of Minn., 1974).
9. M. Norman, "Substitutes for Mother," *Human Behavior* (February 1978): 18-22.
10. A. Toffler, *Future Shock* (New York: Bantam, 1970).
11. E. Jennings, "Mobiocentric Man," *Psychology Today* (July 1970): 36.
12. H. I. Smith, "Sex and Singleness the Second Time Around," *Christianity Today* (May 25, 1979): 16-22.
13. H. G. Zeroff, *Finding Intimacy* (New York: Random, 1978), p. 37.
14. G. L. Engel, "Sudden and Rapid Death During Psychological Stress: Folklore or Folk Wisdom?, *Annals of Internal Medicine* 74 (1971): 771-82.
15. B. MacMahon and T. F. Pugh, "Suicide in the Widowed," *American Journal of Epidemiology* 81 (1965): 23.
16. E. Kübler-Ross, *On Death and Dying* (New York: Macmillan, 1969).

Chapter 8

1. These approaches to thought managment are adapted from P. M. Lewinsohn, R. F. Munoz, M. A. Youngren, and A. M. Zeiss, *Control Your Depression* (Englewood Cliffs, N.J.: Prentice-Hall, 1978), and J. Young, "A Cognitive-Behavioral Approach to the Treatment of Loneliness" (paper presented at the UCLA Research Conference on Loneliness, Los Angeles, May 1979). Young is at the Center for Cognitive Therapy, University of Pennsylvania.
2. This happens to be the title of a recent book by J. Johnson (Chicago: Moody, 1979).
3. D. Phillips, *How to Fall Out of Love* (Boston: Houghton Mifflin, 1978).
4. M. L. West, *The Devil's Advocate* (New York: Dell, 1969), pp. 334-35.

Chapter 9

1. The suggestions regarding shy people are adapted in part from P. G. Zimbardo, *Shyness: What It Is and What to Do about It* and P. M. Lewinsohn, et al., *Control Your Depression*.

2. I. Altman and D. A. Taylor, *Social Penetration: The Development of Interpersonal Relationships* (New York: Holt, Rinehart, & Winston, 1973).
3. Parts of this section are adapted from S. Miller, E. W. Nunnally, and D. B. Wackman, *Alive and Aware* (Minneapolis: Interpers. Commun., 1975).
4. C. M. Whipple, Jr., and D. Whittle, *The Compatibility Test* (Englewood Cliffs, N.J.: Prentice-Hall, 1976).
5. Ibid.
6. J. J. Swihart, *How Do I Say I Love You?* (Downers Grove, Ill.: InterVarsity, 1977).
7. H. J. Clinebell and C. H. Clinebell, *The Intimate Marriage* (New York: Harper & Row, 1970), pp. 54-55.
8. E. E. Ford and R. L. Zorn, *Why Be Lonely?*, pp. 52-58.

Chapter 10
1. I am indebted to Joyce Thomas, assistant dean of academic affairs, Spring Arbor College, for this provocative perspective on loss, and for a number of helpful suggestions on aiding widows, all stemming from her work with widows in "Life Management" groups held in cooperation with funeral homes in the Owosso, Michigan, area.
2. R. E. Kavanaugh, *Facing Death* (Baltimore: Penguin, 1974), pp. 105-24.
3. Adapted from an approach to grief therapy proposed by Edgar Jackson, cited in David Dempsey, *The Way We Die* (New York: McGraw-Hill, 1975), pp. 158-60.
4. Ibid., p. 161.
5. E. M. Duvall, *Marriage and Family Development*, 5th ed. (New York: Lippincott, 1977).
6. J. S. Turner and D. B. Helms, *Contemporary Adulthood* (Philadelphia: Saunders, 1979), p. 201.

Chapter 11
1. Psalm 139:1-10, 13, 15-16.
2. G. E. W. Scobie, *Psychology of Religion* (London: Batsford, 1975).
3. C. W. Ellison and R. F. Paloutzian, "Religious Experience and Quality of Life" (paper presented at the annual meeting of the American Psychological Association, New York, September 1979). Also, R. F. Paloutzian and C. W. Ellison, "Loneliness and Quality of Life," to be published in L. A. Peplau and D. Perlman, *Loneliness: A Sourcebook of Current Theory, Research, and Therapy* (New York: Wiley-Interscience).
4. C. W. Ellison, "Secularism in the Sanctuary" (unpublished manuscript).
5. S. Rogers and J. Rogers, *The Family Together: Intergenerational Education in the Church School* (Los Angeles: Acton House, 1976).